ASHE Higher Education Report: Volume 31, Number 2
Adrianna J. Kezar, Kelly Ward, Lisa E. Wolf-Wendel, Series Editors

The Uses of Institutional Culture

*Strengthening Identification and Building
Brand Equity in Higher Education*

J. Douglas Toma, Greg Dubrow, and
Matthew Hartley

The Uses of Institutional Culture: Strengthening Identification and Building Brand Equity in Higher Education

J. Douglas Toma, Greg Dubrow, Matthew Hartley

ASHE Higher Education Report: Volume 31, Number 2

Adrianna J. Kezar, Kelly Ward, Lisa Wolf-Wendel, Series Editors

ISSN 1551-6970   electronic ISSN 1554-6306   ISBN 0-7879-8124-9

The ASHE Higher Education Report is part of the Jossey-Bass Higher and Adult Education Series and is published six times a year by Wiley Subscription Services, Inc., A Wiley Company, at Jossey-Bass, 989 Market Street, San Francisco, California 94103-1741.

For subscription information, see the Back Issue/Subscription Order Form in the back of this volume.

CALL FOR PROPOSALS: Prospective authors are strongly encouraged to contact Kelly Ward (kaward@wsu.edu) or Lisa Wolf-Wendel (lwolf@ku.edu). See "About the ASHE Higher Education Report Series" in the back of this volume.

Visit the Jossey-Bass Web site at **www.josseybass.com.**

Printed in the United States of America on acid-free recycled paper.

Advisory Board

ASHE

The ASHE Higher Education Report Series is sponsored by the Association for the Study of Higher Education (ASHE), which provides an editorial advisory board of ASHE members.

Contents

Executive Summary

A strong institutional culture has concrete uses in universities and colleges: culture is not simply something that is but is something that can do. In connecting people and institutions, institutional culture can pay real dividends, particularly in external relations and in building the campus community that is so critical in student affairs, but also in managing administrative and academic units. This monograph thus explores the particular set of benefits accrued by institutions that do what is necessary to enjoy a strong set of institutional norms, values, and beliefs, which is how we define culture.

This book moves beyond the common conception of institutional culture as simply binding together those who work and learn at institutions of higher education, extending the discussion to explore the "so what?" question. It explores how institutional culture enables a university or college community, broadly defined, to identify with the institution. It also examines how that culture helps to clarify the image of that institution in ways that bring what those in marketing would call "brand equity." Through driving institutional identification and brand equity, institutional culture has real uses in strategy and management in higher education, including in external relations and in involving the campus-based community more deeply in the life of the campus. Each is, the authors argue, about using institutional culture in strategic ways.

The authors explore these three concepts of institutional identification, brand equity, and institutional culture—and particularly the broad intersections among them—toward an appreciation of how institutions can use what they yield in strategy and management. Academic or administrative units are much better positioned to be effective when those within them have a concrete appreciate of the norms, values, and beliefs of the institution (institutional culture), relate their own fortunes with those of the institution (institutional identification), and can represent the image of the institution in ways that yield benefits for it (brand equity).

Institutional identification, as an idea, has yet to be widely applied in the context of higher education. The notion is straightforward: people want to associate with places they view as distinctive, central, and enduring and want to know that others view them the same way. Stronger identification, the authors argue, results from stronger institutional culture: people must understand what the institution is about before they are likely to identify with it. Thus, strengthening institutional culture has discernable benefits; culture is, once again, not just something to have but is more accurately something to use. Institutional identification produces outcomes. Writing on the topic suggests that people who identify strongly are more apt to seek more contact with the organization, to cooperate with other members of the organization, to direct competitive behavior toward outsiders, and to be more active and loyal relative to the organization.

The authors also contend that clarifying the image of an institution, in marketing parlance "a brand," depends on institutional culture—the extended university community's having a concrete sense of the norms, values, and beliefs of a university or college. Again, the focus is on the uses of institutional culture, and the value of a brand is identified as just such a use. Those who write about marketing describe the value of a brand in terms of equity in it. Brand equity, as applied to higher education, includes awareness of an institution, recognition of what an institution is known for, a sense of loyalty toward the institution, an understanding of the worth of the institution, and the desire to pay a premium price to be associated with it.

This book does not ask directly what creates a strong brand in higher education or address how specifically institutions might strengthen identification; instead, it focuses on the likely tangible benefits that come with the institutional identification and brand equity that institutional culture drives. The bottom line is that an institution benefits when constituents not only know it but also associate it with positive attributes. Institutions, then, do not build institutional culture for its own sake. They do so to heighten the identification and clarify the image that creates the connections between constituents and institutions that are, once again, exactly the goal of those working in student affairs, managing academic and administrative units, and overseeing external relations at American universities and colleges.

After discussing institutional identification and brand equity, the authors turn to institutional culture. Their review of institutional culture provides examples of what enhances institutional identification and brand equity. They describe institutional culture in a simple framework, focusing on its substance—an institution's norms, values, and beliefs—and the concrete forms that culture assumes. These forms include the tangible symbols, language, narratives, and practices needed to express the understandings that are common across an organization—elements that can be measured as opposed to the more intangible (or inherently intangible) substance of institutional culture.

The authors contend, therefore, that brand equity, institutional identification, and institutional culture are mutually reinforcing. As brands strengthen, so does perceived organizational identity and construed external image (the markers of institutional identification) as people want to associate with esteemed institutions. Thus, the benefits of brand equity and institutional identification are circular: stronger brands lead to more identification and vice versa. And a robust institutional culture is essential to bring the clarity of a message that is a prerequisite for both institutional identification and brand equity. Institutions must understand themselves before members can rally around their purposes and aspirations and before a campus can frame itself to be appealing to outsiders. Therefore, through institutional identification and brand equity, institutional culture has real uses for universities and colleges.

The book concludes by inviting institutions themselves to consider what they can do to enhance the shared ideals and frames of reference that mark any organization. This call includes, of course, strengthening the tangible forms and less tangible substance of culture that members of an institutional community can use to understand and express what their institution means.

Foreword

Robert Zemsky recently argued that higher education institutions face an identity crisis. Institutional missions have shifted, and more and more institutions of higher education that once served fairly distinctive missions have become more and more alike (termed *institutional isomorphism*). This phenomenon, he believes, harms institutions, because they no longer serve well-established missions and have no particular market niche. Institutional isomorphism results in a public policy problem—by not meeting state priorities and goals—and a marketing problem—by potentially affecting student enrollments. Mission shift also has less obvious effects. For example, members of the institution (faculty, staff, students, and alumni) may no longer have as strong an affiliation. People identify with a clear mission and sense of identity. Often employees are drawn to places that are distinctive and reflect their values. Moreover, as institutional missions change, long-time employees—faculty and staff—lose a sense of how to conduct their roles effectively. Alumni no longer feel an affiliation with the school. Higher education institutions may also become less competitive in the face of for-profit competition, which has been effective in creating market niches. The possible problems are manifold. This significant, systemic problem in higher education is the focus of this important monograph, *The Uses of Institutional Culture*.

Toma, Dubrow, and Hartley provide a compelling case for how institutions can become more distinctive and thereby create market niches and brands, as Zemsky suggests. The authors provide practical tools for how institutions can shift their institutional cultures, which they see as the main tool for creating institutional distinctiveness. Marketing has often been considered a taboo topic in higher education because it is associated with the business world and higher education institutions do not see their students as customers. The authors of this book, however, make a case that business concepts and marketing can be used constructively and with integrity as a way to ensure that an institution is meeting its established mission. An institution uses marketing to promote and make visible its identity. Many higher education institutions have currently lost their sense of identity. By taking a marketing perspective, institutions can examine and reflect on their identities and help define what image they want to promote and then move the institution toward that vision as well. As the institution begins to move toward this vision, it can promote itself as a particular brand. The authors demonstrate the interrelationship of brand, institutional identification, and institutional culture. Through the branding process, the culture is changed, and through the alteration of institutional culture, the brand is created. These two symbiotic processes can help institutions in crisis, or those that are simply afloat, to rethink their operations and to once again become successful.

The authors do caution that image and reality must correspond. Again, the fear of higher education institutions' using business technique and metaphors is the dark side that can emerge from these concepts. Image has at times been used in an illusory way in business to sell a product that is different from reality. The authors stress that they argue for image in the best sense—as a vision for propelling an institution forward and to change in ways that are beneficial for the community. They review the benefits of branding and institutional identification, making a strong case for why higher education institutions should think carefully about these concepts. Readers will benefit from a detailed review of the meaning and practice of institutional culture and identification and the concept of branding. Toma, Dubrow, and Hartley use powerful case studies of higher education institutions that have successfully branded their institutions or created strong employee identification. This publication will be of particular interest to enrollment management officers, admissions and development staff, alumni affairs offices, and other members of the higher education community who are working to create connections with students, alumni, and other external constituents. In addition, those in academic and student affairs can use the ideas in this monograph to enhance employee identification, morale, and satisfaction.

Adrianna Kezar
Series Editor

Acknowledgments

We would like to thank Adrianna Kezar, editor of the ASHE series, for her considerable patience and helpful counsel, both substantive and technical, as we completed this monograph. Thanks also to Lisa Wolf-Wendel and Kelly Ward, the new editors of the series, for shepherding the manuscript through the final steps in the process to publication. Each is a valued colleague and good friend, and we wish Kelly and Lisa the very best as they begin their work as editors. We would also like to thank the several colleagues nationally who served as referees for this monograph. Their efforts greatly improved our approach to this topic.

Our project began at the University of Pennsylvania, where Matt is appointed and we were each affiliated at the time, enjoying the support of our good colleagues and students there. Doug would also like to thank his Penn colleagues and students affiliated with the Executive Doctorate in Higher Education Management as well as his present colleagues and students at the Institute of Higher Education at the University of Georgia. Greg would like to extend the same thanks to his colleagues at Florida International University.

Finally, we would like to acknowledge the contributions of our various families and friends, particularly Doug's wife, Linda, and Matt's wife, Jenny.

Identification, Equity, and Culture

INSTITUTIONAL CULTURE MATTERS IN HIGHER EDUCA-
TION, and universities and colleges commonly express the need to
strengthen their culture. A strong culture is perceived, correctly so, to engender a needed sense of connectedness between and among the varied constituents associated with a campus. Linking organizational culture and social
cohesion is not a novel concept. (We use the terms *organizational culture* and
institutional culture interchangeably throughout our discussion.) Our primary
contribution here is to argue that a strong institutional culture has concrete
uses in universities and colleges: culture is not simply something that is but
is something that can do. In connecting people and institutions, institutional
culture can pay real dividends, particularly in external relations and in building the campus community that is so critical in student affairs, but also in
managing administrative and academic units. Institutional culture is not just
something to have, which is where the discussion of the concept usually
focuses, but is something to use.

We thus explore the particular set of benefits accrued by institutions
that do what is necessary to enjoy a strong set of institutional norms, values,
and beliefs, which is how we define culture. We move beyond the common
conception of institutional culture's simply binding together those who
work and learn at our institutions of higher education, extending the discussion to explore the "so what?" question. We explore how institutional
culture enables a university or college community, broadly defined, to identify with the institution. We also examine how it helps clarify the image of
that institution in ways that bring what those in marketing would call

"brand equity." Through driving institutional identification and brand equity, institutional culture has real uses in strategy and management in higher education.

Institutions devote considerable attention to framing strategies intended to develop relations with external constituents, connecting them more directly with the life and fate of the campus. A strong institutional culture yields the institutional identification and brand equity that encourages successful external relations. The support of these members of the extended institutional community is of paramount importance because it is they who provide needed resources, whether through donations or legislative appropriations. External constituents also contribute to the construction and maintenance of an institution's reputation—a less tangible but still significant resource. Accordingly, when external constituents view an institution as "their" university or college, the result for that campus is desirable. Scholars addressing higher education have tended to examine the complex roles of culture in organizations without extending their analyses to describe how culture creates advantages in the external marketplace by encouraging strong identification and clear brand and the benefits that accompany them. Generating just such identification and image is the essence of external relations in higher education.

The same is true, of course, of involving the campus-based community more deeply in the life of the campus: it is about using institutional culture in strategic ways. Potency and clarity in culture, identification, and image tend to yield a robust community on campus. As just one example, the essence of student affairs in higher education is just this encouragement of community. Further, academic or administrative units are much better positioned to be effective when those within them have a concrete appreciation of the institution's norms, values, and beliefs (institutional culture), relate their own fortunes with those of the institution (institutional identification), and can represent the institution's image in ways that yield benefits for it (brand equity). We explore these three concepts—and particularly the broad intersections among them—toward an appreciation of how institutions can use what they yield in strategy and management.

Institutional Identification

Institutional identification, as an idea, has yet to be widely applied in the context of higher education. The notion is straightforward: people want to associate with places they view as distinctive, central, and enduring and where they know others view them the same way. Dutton, Dukerich, and Harquail (1994) term what people know about their own institutions "perceived organizational identity" and what they perceive others to know "construed external image." As these images grow more positive, identification with a university or college is enhanced, and individuals can assume for themselves the positive attributes associated with the institution. The self-concept of those who support an institution comes to parallel the characteristics that they believe define the university or college.

Stronger identification results from stronger institutional culture: people must understand what the institution is about before they are likely to identify with it. Thus, strengthening institutional culture has discernable benefits; that is, culture is not just something to have, but is more accurately something to use. Enhanced connectedness results in support for the campus, both internally and externally, in tangible and intangible ways. In other words, the more people, whatever or how direct their association with a university or college might be, who associate their own fortunes with those of an institution, the better it is for that institution. Institutional identification, as a concept, is therefore the link between having culture and using culture. It is the tangible result of a strong culture, facilitating the closely related concepts of community and connectedness. The building of these concepts is exactly the goal of those in student affairs, in management of academic and administrative work, and in external relations who must consider daily how constituents, both external and internal, feel about and act toward the institution.

That overarching goal is clarified by framing it in terms of institutional culture, and then culture as strategy. Thus, the usually theoretical concept focuses on its applied aspects. The discussion begins by exploring institutional identification. The common approach to institutional culture in higher education is to argue that it fosters a sense of "oneness with or belonging to" a university or college as an organization. We agree. But we go the additional step of suggesting how the institutional identification that strong culture engenders has real utility for higher education institutions, as it does for all organizations. Institutional identification produces outcomes. People who identify strongly are more apt to seek more contact with the organization, to cooperate with other members of the organization, to direct competitive behavior toward outsiders, and to be more active and loyal relative to the organization.

Brand Equity

We also extend the notion of the benefits of people connecting with institutions through institutional culture—the institutional identification that comes with a strong culture—through next exploring the concept of brand equity. Clarifying the image of an institution, what in marketing parlance is called "a brand," depends on the extended university community's having a concrete sense of the institution's norms, values, and beliefs. Again, we focus on the uses of institutional culture, identifying the value of a brand as just such a use.

Those who write about marketing describe the value of a brand in terms of equity in it, and we believe the concept extends neatly, as well as necessarily, to higher education, where it has yet to be broadly applied. Brand equity, as applied to higher education, includes awareness of an institution, recognition of what an institution is known for, a sense of loyalty toward the institution, an understanding of the institution's worth, and the desire to pay a premium price to be associated with it. Aaker (1991) defines brand equity as the value that comes from having a name or symbol that differentiates the services of one provider from another. Certain names and symbols have a special mystique; whether the name is Harvard, Mercedes-Benz, or Mt. Fuji, brand equity is linked with closely related notions such as image, reputation, status, and prestige. And nonprofit organizations, including colleges and universities, have as much interest in developing a clear image as for-profit corporations. Through a mix of information and aura, the names and symbols that express image communicate quickly what the institution wants people to know about it and its products.

It is essential to remember, however, that image and reality must correspond. A well-cultivated image will reap nothing but ridicule unless it reflects the substance of the organization: image must reflect culture. Image must also be tied to an institution's mission and vision—its fundamental purposes and significant ambitions—to be clear. If an institution is unclear about why it is here, it will not only struggle in framing an image but also have difficulty expressing the norms, values, and beliefs that make up its organizational culture and are the foundation of institutional identification. How can an institution expect outsiders to know what matters within it and what makes it special and important if the institution itself does not really know? Thus, brand and culture must connect with each other—and with the idea of mission—if a university or college is to derive equity from its image.

That said, we are not asking directly here what creates a strong brand in higher education; instead, we focus on the likely tangible benefits—awareness, associations, loyalty, perceived quality (brand equity), contact, cooperation, attachment, and loyalty (institutional identification)—that come with the institutional identification and brand equity that institutional culture drives. The bottom line is that an institution benefits when constituents not only know it but also associate it with positive attributes. Institutions, then, do not build institutional culture for its own sake. They do so to heighten the identification and clarify the image that creates the connections between constituents and institutions that are, once again, exactly the goal of those working in student affairs, managing academic and administrative units, and participating in external relations at American universities and colleges.

Institutional Culture

After discussing institutional identification and brand equity, we turn to institutional culture, both in substance and through form, given that is how institutional identification—what is distinctive, central, and enduring about an organization—is expressed and heightened. Through reviewing institutional culture, we provide examples of what enhances institutional identification and brand equity. We describe institutional culture within a simple framework, focusing on its substance—an institution's norms, values, and beliefs—and the concrete forms that culture assumes. They include the tangible symbols, language, narratives, and practices needed to express the understandings common across an organization—elements that can be measured as opposed to the more intangible (or inherently intangible) substance of institutional culture.

Our definition of institutional culture builds on the work of Tierney (1988), Kuh and Whitt (1988), and Schein (1992). Institutional culture consists of the shared beliefs, values, assumptions, and ideologies that bind a group together. At universities and colleges, institutional culture conveys a sense of identity (who we are), facilitates commitment (what we stand for), enhances stability (how we do things around here), guides sense making (how we understand events), and defines authority (who is influential) (Kuh and Whitt, 1988). Tierney (1988), using Geertz's metaphor (1973), describes organizational culture as an "interconnected web" and notes that its presence is most apparent when a member violates a group's codes and standards.

In the following discussion, we thus build on the 1988 ASHE-ERIC Higher Education Report by Kuh and Whitt, *The Invisible Tapestry: Culture in American Colleges and Universities*. We explore how organizational culture promotes identification with an institution, encouraging individuals to view their college or university as set apart—distinctive, important, and lasting. We connect institutional identification with the equity in a respected brand that also results from a well-developed institutional culture. Again, both are key to developing a strong campus community and the effective external relations that are so highly sought after in American higher education. They are the uses of institutional culture—the ability to draw people into campus life and cause them to want to support "their" esteemed institution.

Using Institutional Culture

Thus, we contend that brand equity, institutional identification, and institutional culture are mutually reinforcing. As brands strengthen, so does perceived organizational identity and construed external image (the markers of institutional identification), as people want to associate with esteemed institutions. So the benefits of brand equity and institutional identification are circular: stronger brands lead to more identification and vice versa. And a robust institutional culture is essential to bring the clarity of message that is prerequisite for both institutional identification and brand equity. Institutions must understand themselves before members can rally around their purposes and aspirations and before a campus can frame itself to be appealing to outsiders. We thus establish the uses of institutional culture through institutional identification and brand equity.

We conclude by inviting institutions themselves to consider what they can do to enhance the shared ideals and frames of reference that mark any organization, which include strengthening the tangible forms of culture—symbols, language, narratives, and practices—that members of an institutional community can use to understand and express what their institution means. In the end, it is what makes otherwise similar institutions distinctive in both the eyes of their key constituents and in the eyes of outsiders.

Such distinctiveness is precisely the raw material of institutional identification. It is also what goes into building a strong brand, whether in the corporate world or in higher education. The most effective organizations and institutions are exactly those that use a strong internal culture to express their distinctive, central, and enduring natures most effectively (Chaudhuri, 2002; Fombrun, 1996, Garbett, 1988). In other words, the best performing (which does not necessarily mean the most prestigious) institutions typically have well-defined norms, values, and beliefs and clear symbols, language, narratives, and practices to articulate them. Accordingly, they enjoy tangible benefits, building actual equity in their brand.

Doing so has become increasingly important in American higher education, given increasing pressures related to market forces. Bok (1986) suggests that the characteristic features of American higher education are autonomy, competitiveness, and responsiveness. Although colleges and universities are generally free to pursue their aspirations, they exist in a highly competitive and crowded environment (Toma, 2003). Institutions must convince tuition-paying students (or their parents), private donors, and state legislators (if public) that they are worthy of support. These characteristics make building institutional identification—both internally (with students) and externally (with alumni)—and enhancing the equity that comes with a strong brand so critical.

Some have sought to establish their legitimacy and status through isomorphism, mimicking market leaders (Glynn and Abzug, 2002; Labianca and others, 2001; Scott, 2001). The competitive advantage that market leaders have in reputation and resources, however, often makes "follow the leader" an exercise in frustration. In fact, the marketplace tends to reward institutions that differentiate themselves (Clark, 1987; Zemsky, Shaman, and Iannozzi, 1997). A distinctive image that accurately reflects institutional priorities and programmatic emphases is a valuable competitive advantage. Unlike businesses, institutions cannot always distinguish themselves on the basis of price, so using institutional culture to build identification and brand becomes even more important.

Finally, institutional effectiveness also results from the confluence of identification, brand, and culture. Fairfield-Sonn (2001) notes that culture matters in organizations because it increases organizational performance and the external orientation of organizations; culture, once again, has uses (Wilkins and Ouchi, 1983). But it is important to remember that institutional culture is distinct from institutional climate. An examination of the latter might use quantitative measures to focus on issues such as employee satisfaction or student attitudes, intending to use survey research to provide a snapshot of shared subjective experiences in order to assess organizational effectiveness (Schneider, Bowen, Ehrhart, and Holcombe, 2000; Schein, 2000). Research on organizational culture is usually qualitative, seeking to develop a deep understanding of how people experience their professional lives. We focus here on organizational culture, arguing that the institutional identification and brand equity that accompany strong culture have important operational implications by building campus community and by enhancing external relations.

An Illustration: Tusculum College

To illustrate the importance of the uses of institutional culture on a campus—the confluence of institutional identification, brand equity, and the substance and forms of institutional culture—we present the case of Tusculum College (drawn from Hartley's study [2002] of mission-centered change at small colleges). We invite you to consider Tusculum throughout our discussion; the case is used to illustrate several points below. Bear in mind how, by strengthening institutional culture, Tusculum enhanced awareness, associations, loyalty, and perceived quality (the markers of brand equity) and began to realize the benefits of stronger institutional identification. In other words, think about how Tusculum did not just build institutional culture but also positioned itself to use it.

Scene One

Imagine you are a successful businessperson in a small city in the South. One afternoon you receive a call from the president's office of Tusculum College in nearby Greeneville. You know very little about the institution. It's one of several small colleges in the area. When you've driven by, external appearances suggest a typical liberal arts institution with stone and brick buildings bedecked in ivy arranged around an oak-crowned quad. It turns out that the president would like to meet with you. You agree. Later that day, you mention the call to a coworker, who refers to the institution disparagingly as "that Yankee college." (Apparently, many of its students are recruited from the Northeast.) Another coworker remarks, "Tusculum College is in Greeneville but not of Greeneville."

The following week, the president and the vice president for institutional advancement come to your office. "Tusculum College is the oldest college in the state and the oldest coeducational college related to the Presbyterian Church (U.S.A.). Our mission is to provide our students with a well-rounded education and to prepare them for successful careers. We try to exemplify the ideal of a community of scholars, where students work closely with faculty members." The president goes on to mention several prominent businesspeople who currently serve on Tusculum's board of trustees. His next question takes you aback: "You wouldn't want to be on Tusculum's board, would you?" You demur, saying that you want to learn a bit more about the college first and agree to visit the campus the following Friday.

When you arrive on campus, you are somewhat dismayed to find that what you took for genteel shabbiness is significant deferred maintenance. At least one building on campus is boarded up. Paint is peeling everywhere. Carpets are threadbare. The president takes you on a walking tour of the campus. (You notice he steers you away from the boarded-up building.) You are also struck by how quiet everything is. "Where are the students?" you ask. The president explains that on Friday, many of them go home for the weekend to be with their families.

Despite the president's obvious reluctance, you also meet with a group of faculty members. Initially, they appear reticent. As the conversation continues, it becomes clear that old animosities are barely being held in check. Two of the faculty members won't look at each other. You begin the meeting by explaining that you want to learn all you can about Tusculum because you are considering serving on the board. One faculty member quips, "Well, this is a first. I've never met a board member!" A spirited conversation follows, during which the following statements are made:

We're a small, poor college, but we really care about our students. Still, I worry about our curriculum—a little of this and a little of that. I don't think we're giving them the education they need.

Each department is trying to just stay alive, and there's a lot of competition and bad blood. I've had my share of flaming arrows shot in my butt during faculty meetings.

I know of a lot of faculty members who just come in, teach their courses, and go right home. A lot have other jobs on the side.

Quite frankly, the president has been around for a long time, and he makes up his own mind. It doesn't matter what we do in terms of committee work; the faculty doesn't count for much.

Scene Two

Imagine you are a successful businessperson in a small city in the South. One afternoon you receive a call from the president's office of Tusculum College. It turns out the president would like to meet with you. You agree. You've seen a few articles about Tusculum in the local newspaper and vaguely recall that they have a fairly new president, who is making some big changes there. Later that day, you mention the call to a coworker. He remarks that his niece was just admitted to Tusculum as part of an aggressive local recruiting effort. Another coworker, who lives nearby, mentions that her family has gone to see Tusculum's new football team play several times this fall. "They really know how to make these into great family events," she says.

The following week, the president and the vice president for institutional advancement come to your office. "Tusculum College is the oldest college in the state and the oldest coeducational college related to the Presbyterian Church (U.S.A.). Tusculum is dedicated to promoting the civic arts—those particular qualities and characteristics of mind and heart that make for engaged and productive citizens, in the workplace and in their communities. Come to campus and see what we're doing." You agree to visit the following Friday.

When you arrive on campus, you are somewhat dismayed to find that what you took for genteel shabbiness is significant deferred maintenance. The president takes you on a walking tour of the campus, during which he remarks, "Unfortunately, this great institution has been somewhat neglected. We're doing what we can to fix that." You notice that workers are busy scraping and painting. Some new flowerbeds are being tended. The president takes you past two buildings that are boarded up. "These two buildings have been condemned. We can't use them yet, but one of our priorities in our upcoming capital campaign is to restore them. They will be beautiful and needed as our student enrollment increases."

The campus is bustling with activity. Several students greet the president as he passes. "They're excited because we're playing a big rival tonight in football." The president walks into an academic building and introduces you to a group of faculty members and then graciously excuses himself. A spirited conversation follows, during which the following statements are made:

We're a small, poor college, but we really care about our students. "The civic arts" is the unifying idea for the overall educational experience. The faculty is redesigning the whole curriculum. The new courses focus on issues like social responsibility and civic duty. We're even thinking about switching to a block calendar, where students will take one intensive course at a time so we can do more community-based learning, like service learning.

We have a lot more interactive relationship between the faculty and the administration and the board than we ever did before.

The president has said, "There are lots of small, caring colleges around. If that's our reason for being, we might as well just shut our doors and let you all find institutions that can better suit your needs. But there is a need for something we once were. We were founded on civic republican ideals to help create new leaders—we have a chance to resurrect that mission.

How does the Tusculum case illustrate the uses of institutional culture to strengthen institutional identification and build brand equity? In the second vignette, eighteen months after the first, the college clearly has become more appealing in terms of campus community, and thus attractive to external constituents such as the prospective board member in the vignettes. Even then, Tusculum College still faces prodigious fiscal challenges. It needs to address flagging enrollments, a meager base of philanthropic support, a potentially crippling amount of deferred maintenance, and more—problems that will take far longer than eighteen months to address. But the institution is moving forward. It has clarified its mission: a common purpose leading to a new vision expressed through initiatives such as a curricular change and a new football team. Doing so has resulted in the formation and rediscovery of norms, values, and beliefs—the substance of institutional culture. Tusculum has become more collegial, more open, and more accountable. It has also established and reestablished ways to express this institutional culture.

In the second vignette, the institution's norms, values, and beliefs have become clearer and more dynamic. The Tusculum community has come to value again a collegiality that had been lost; through its curriculum, it underscores core values of social responsibility and civic duty, and it has come to believe in the institution's prospects. The college is focused on differentiating itself from other institutions through not only a new curriculum but also a newly robust institutional culture around it. The notion of "how we do things around here" has become palpably more positive at the college in just the eighteen months between the vignettes. And Tusculum underscores these new and energized norms, values, and beliefs through symbols, language, narratives, and practices; the forms of institutional culture support its substance. The college has begun to renovate the physical campus, the president has become more of a positive symbolic figure, there is a new confidence in the language with which the institution is introduced, the institution has begun to construct a compelling narrative to represent itself, and the community has begun to come together to celebrate the institution.

In doing so, Tusculum increasingly underscores what is distinctive, central, and enduring about the institution—the definition of institutional identification. The campus community has come to recognize what is good about the institution and that others are beginning to recognize it as well. The resulting increase in identification with the institution is likely to have a positive payoff, that strengthening institutional culture will likely pay dividends. The Tusculum brand has also improved, and it is reasonable to expect benefits to accrue to an institution with increased value in its brand: brand loyalty, brand awareness, perceived quality, and brand associations. Even with the changes over the eighteen months between the two vignettes, Tusculum still struggles financially. But through active development of a stronger culture and with the resulting institutional identification and brand equity, Tusculum finds itself in a much better position to build campus community and enhance external relations.

At Tusculum, as elsewhere in higher education, culture does not exist in a vacuum. It has real uses at universities and colleges. After considering these vignettes, it is not difficult to determine which Tusculum a donor would rather support or prospective student would rather attend. The emergent organizational culture has a much greater potential to draw external constituents to the institution and energize the campus community (Hartley, 2002). They can better identify with the institution and are thus more inclined to involve themselves with it. And Tusculum is a long way toward establishing the equity that comes with a strong brand.

Here are the uses of institutional culture: leveraging institutional identification and brand equity into support for the institution's overall missions and ambitions (Toma, 2003). The desired end of institutional culture is not just to have it but to cause people to want to associate with a university or college—to endorse it by engaging with and contributing to the institution, including tangible support through tuition, donations, and appropriations. The essence of student affairs, administrative and academic units, and external relations in American higher education is to advance the congruence of institutional goals with the goals of individuals who are associated with the institution. Developing a strong institutional culture is of paramount importance.

Using Culture to Strengthen Institutional Identification

INDIVIDUALS IDENTIFY WITH UNIVERSITIES AND COLLEGES, in part, because institutions represent societal values. Higher education institutions have such deep significance for people because they are so closely related with such deeply held American ideals as progress and success. They also represent the self-made person who is so greatly valued in American society: someone who has achieved in a highly competitive system (Toma, 2003).

Accordingly, universities and colleges have long used civic pride and the expression of community and national values to advance their interests. Institutions have long exploited the perception that having a successful higher education institution in a given community announces to the world that that community is successful as well. Whether in constructing campus buildings and supporting academic programs or even supporting university sports teams, communities have long been willing to do whatever it takes to ensure success. Boosters have refused to be outdone by others, building lavish campuses, even in remote outposts. What one local institution has others need to have, and competition has only become more intense over time, even when some institutions have considerably more resources and other advantages (Toma, 2003).

Factors such as national values and local pride explain why local communities identify with higher education institutions, supporting them handsomely as a rule. The degree to which individuals identify with "their" institution, as with any organization, is a product of two elements. The first is what they believe is distinctive, central, and enduring about the organization—their "perceived organizational identity." The second is what they believe others think about the institution—their "construed external image" (Dutton, Dukerich, and Harquail, 1994, p. 239.) Both of these constructs are linked with national values and local pride (Toma, 2003).

But identification is also linked with the institutional culture that is so important in making institutions understandable and accessible to constituents, underscoring what is distinctive, central, and enduring about an institution. Institutional culture works in conjunction with national values and local pride for external constituents and is likely the dominant driver of institutional identification for those on campus, whether students, faculty, administrators, or staff. Institutional identification is very much a factor of institutional culture: an institution's norms, values, and beliefs as articulated through more concrete symbols, language, narratives, and practices. They are what cause individuals to use the attribute they believe defines the institution to also define themselves.

Identifying with Institutions

When people identify strongly with a university or college—when the self-concept of individuals assumes many of the same characteristics that they understand define a particular organization as a social group—benefits accrue to that institution and the individuals alike. Dutton, Dukerich, and Harquail (1994) offer the illustration of a 3M Corporation salesman: "I found out today that it is a lot easier being a salesman for 3M than for a little jobber no one has ever heard of. When you don't have to waste time justifying your existence or explaining why you are here, it gives you a certain amount of self-assurance. And, I discovered I came across warmer and friendlier. It made me feel good and enthusiastic to be 'somebody' for a change" (p. 239). The 3M salesman views himself as innovative and successful, which is how he understands the 3M organization and how he understands others to view 3M. "Organizational membership can confer positive attributes on its members, and people may feel proud to belong to an organization that is believed to have socially valued characteristics" (Dutton, Dukerich, and Harquail, 1994, p. 240). It is thus natural that the 3M salesman has a strong degree of identification with the organization.

How strongly someone like the salesman identifies with an organization reflects the degree to which his or her self-concept is tied to his or her organizational membership: "When organizational identification is strong, a member's self-concept has incorporated a large part of what he or she believes is distinctive, central, and enduring about the organization into what he or she believes is distinctive, central, and enduring about him[self] or herself. When organizational identification is strong . . . other identities in the self-concept have receded, and organizational membership is a central and frequently used basis for self-definition" (Dutton, Dukerich, and Harquail, 1994, p. 242). In other words, institutional members who identify strongly with institutions use these institutions, in large part, to define who they are. The benefits of having those associated with an organization view themselves this way, in terms of the organization itself, are obvious. Such attachments are exactly the goal of those engaged in student affairs, academic and administrative units, and external relations at higher education institutions.

The strength and intensity of identification is also a product of how distinctive or prestigious particular groups are perceived to be. For instance, if a university or college rates highly in the annual *U.S. News & World Report* rankings, individuals can claim the prestige that accompanies this ranking and claim the positive attributes that lead to the ranking for themselves. In the same way, when a sports team wins the conference championship, its supporters perceive themselves to be champions. In short, those who choose to affiliate with an institution can attach themselves to what is perceived to be notable about that institution. Whetten and Mackey (2002) explore these connections between identification and reputation (Keller, 2003; Fombrun and Rindova, 2000; Dukerich and Carter, 2000). Tusculum demonstrates that distinctiveness; its civic arts curriculum goes a long way toward causing people to identify with the institution, thus enhancing the local prestige of the campus for people like the prospective board member.

Institutional identification, then, is the process by which organizational goals and the goals of individuals become increasingly integrated and congruent, a particularly desirable outcome for any organization (Ravasi and van Rekom, 2003; Beyer, Hannah, and Milton, 2000; Adler and Adler, 1988; Hall, Schneider, and Nygren, 1970). The two organizational images—perceived organizational identity and construed external image—thus "influence the cognitive connection that members create with their organization and the kinds of behavior that follow" (Dutton, Dukerich, and Harquail, 1994, p. 239). Accordingly, connections and the behaviors they engender have tangible uses for organizations, including higher education institutions. When constituents identify with organizations, they are more inclined to be involved and responsive, working (and even sacrificing) in conjunction with others in service of the institution's mission, vision, and goals. Consider how the Tusculum faculty became more engaged with the college when they sensed that the new curriculum centered on civic responsibility caused the institution to be more distinctive, central, and enduring. After so long, they had reasons to identify with the college again.

Institutional culture, as the means through which individuals understand organizations, is crucial in building these connections. Indeed, building identification is one of the key roles of culture in an organization. Culture provides constant and tangible reminders of what is distinctive, central, and enduring about an organization. Again, culture is not simply present in organizations: it exists for real purposes. Collins and Porras (1996) write about strong ideologies embedded in strong cultures that lead to the enduring businesses that are so highly regarded (Collins, 2001).

Framing Institutional Identification

Theorists differ on how to frame institutional identification as a concept. Dutton, Dukerich, and Harquail (1994) provide a good starting point, suggesting that the attractiveness of an organization is a product of three elements, each of which is associated with self-definition: self-continuity, self-distinctiveness, and self-enhancement. Each element is central to how Americans relate to universities and colleges in general; each is connected with and fostered by institutional culture at these institutions.

Self-continuity is the fit between organizational values and characteristics and the values and characteristics of people associated with them (Dutton, Dukerich, and Harquail, 1994). When the fit between organizations and individuals is strongest, when it occurs over time and across situations, institutional identification is strongest. The same is true when people perceive institutional culture to represent the societal values that have the most significance to them. Thus, a curriculum based on the civic arts is likely to appeal to faculty who view their role as advancing the public good through their teaching and other work. Self-continuity is likely to be strong at institutions closely related to a religious denomination among members of that denomination; their own values and the values of the institution are shaped by a given religious tradition. It may also be pronounced at a land-grant university among the people of the state, most of whom are likely to believe in the institution's applied research, economic development, and related missions.

Self-distinctiveness is the link between the need for people to accentuate their distinctiveness and the perceived distinctiveness of the organization relative to other organizations (Dutton, Dukerich, and Harquail, 1994). Greater perceived distinctiveness leads to greater institutional identification, and a robust institutional culture is all about underscoring distinctiveness, both in substance and in form. Institutional prestige is certainly helpful here, but a strong culture transcends prestige (even though prestigious institutions tend to have strong cultures). Any institution can have pronounced and defined norms, values, and beliefs that it makes understandable through various cultural forms such as symbols. Consider how the distinctive curriculum at Tusculum made the difference in energizing the faculty, causing them to renew their identification with the institution. Humphreys and Brown (2002) explore the importance of personal and shared narratives linked with higher education institutions in encouraging identification.

Self-enhancement is also associated with organizational attractiveness and thus institutional identification. The more an organization's image enhances the self-esteem of someone associated with it, the more that person will identify with that organization (Dutton, Dukerich, and Harquail, 1994) in terms of how they view the organization and how they understand others as viewing the organization. Certainly, supporting a leading institution enhances self-esteem, but so does identifying with an institution that is "in the same league" as the best (and the latter is an important aspect of American higher education) (Bergami and Bagozzi, 2000). The same is true of being affiliated with an institution, like Tusculum, that both insiders and outsiders perceive to be "on the move" (self-enhancement), particularly in ways that enhance its distinctiveness (self-distinctiveness) and conform with the values of the extended college community (self-continuity).

O'Reilly and Chatman (1986) argue that the psychological attachment of individuals to organizations—and thus their involvement in an activity such as donating to a fundraising campaign—is predicated on three foundations: compliance (specific, extrinsic rewards), identification (the desire for affiliation), and internalization (the congruence between individual and organizational values). But Sutton and Harrison (1993) dispute O'Reilly and Chatman's three-dimensional model, suggesting that organization commitment is instead a factor of *affective* commitment (based on values and identification) and *continuance* commitment (based on costs associated with leaving). And Kanter (1972) discusses commitment mechanisms in idealistic organizations somewhat differently still, suggesting that shared sacrifice; commitment of time, energy, and money; renunciation of those outside the group; and communal activities can bring what she calls "institutional transcendence." Albert and Whetten (1985), using universities and churches as illustrations, contend that criteria for organizational identity are a claimed central character, distinctiveness, and temporal continuity. Levinson (1965) uses the notion of "reciprocation" to explore why people relate to certain institutions.

Just as there are various models, there are also several discipline-based approaches to the study of identification with organizations and institutions. Diamond (1993) focuses on organizational identity and organizational affiliation in the context of psychoanalytic theory, exploring the private images people hold of organizations and their various bases and significance. Others focus on the roles of emotion and humor in organizations and institutional identification (Fineman, 1993; Putnam and Mumby, 1993; Kahn, 1989; Van Maanen and Kunda, 1989). Still other work focuses on impression management and audiences (Rosenfeld, Giacalone, and Riordan, 1995; Elsbach and Sutton, 1992; Ginzel, Kramer, and Sutton, 1993). Finally, theory and research on culture and identity generally are instructive (Hatch and Schultz, 2000; Hall, 1990, 1996, 1997; Woodward, 1997; Preston, 1997; Rutherford, 1990; Calhoun, 1987).

Strengthening Institutional Identification

Whatever the model or approach applied, institutional identification is a perception of "oneness with or belonging to" a certain group of other people (Ashworth and Mael, 1989), an insight clarified and strengthened by a robust institutional culture. Institutional culture underscores institution-specific norms, values, and beliefs through more concrete means specific to an institution such as symbols, language, narratives, and practices. These symbols, language, narratives, and practices remind the members of one group how they are distinctive, how they are different from other groups. They do different things, for different people, in different ways, and for different reasons from other groups.

This sense of oneness with or belonging to an institution results from people's self-categorization into groups, allowing them to segment and order the social environment. In doing so, they can define themselves in a given environment—one defined by the institution—while viewing others in terms of that environment and as apart from it. Through choosing to belong to a particular group, people inherently separate themselves from those who identify with other institutions. It is important to remember, however, that people are likely to have multiple institutional affiliations simultaneously (Kuhn and Nelson, 2002) and that organizations themselves have multiple identities with which people relate (Foreman and Whetten, 2002).

Institutional identification thus results from being aware of other groups, perhaps even in competition with them. Indeed, identification can be based in organizational rivalries, such as those between the flagship universities in neighboring states or between competing corporations; rooting against "them" underscores identification with "us" (Toma, 2003). Competition can provide people with even greater incentives to support the institution with which they affiliate, even though some may favor more cooperative approaches and derive identification under those circumstances.

Implicit in the idea of rivalries is that people want to associate with success, which fosters institutional identification. Higher education institutions are such attractive targets for identification, in large part, because of their skill in making plausible claims of being notable. When Tusculum renewed itself, as described in the second vignette, its members could associate with an institution that had clearly articulated purposes and aspirations that people, both insiders and outsiders, could view as significant; the college was beginning to take on an aura of success. But once supporters have experienced success, they expect it in the future. Indeed, at certain universities, success can come to be seen as a birthright and part of the institutional culture. And when matters go wrong or people perceive slippage, repercussions can occur. Moreover, the notion of "disidentification" raised by Bhattacharya and Elsbach (2002) is defined as a sense of separateness as opposed to the cognitive connection associated with identification. Brickson (2000a) discusses separateness in terms of the challenges associated with incorporating diversity research in present conceptual models of institutional identification (Hogg and Terry, 2000).

Associating with success does not require that individuals need to expend direct effort toward the group's goals. It only requires that someone perceive himself or herself as psychologically intertwined with the group's fate. In doing so, people personally experience the group's successes and failures (Rousseau, 1998; Ashforth and Mael, 1989; Mael and Ashforth, 1992; Stern, 1988). In other words, people themselves do not need to attend, have graduated from, or be employed there to identify with a university or college. In fact, some of the most active supporters of American institutions have no direct affiliation, a characteristic commonly manifested through support of campus spectator sports (Toma, 2003).

What matters is the level of exposure that people have to an organization, which enhances the attractiveness of the organization's perceived identity and thus the identification of individuals. In other words, the more contact that people have with a given organization, in terms of both intensity and duration, the more attractive they find the organization and the more they are inclined to identify with the organization (Dutton, Dukerich, and Harquail, 1994). Wiesenfeld, Raghuram, and Garud (2001) explore such notions in their study of organizational identification among virtual workers, suggesting that when work-based social support is high, so is identification. The frequency of interaction with a group is a product of the extent to which people perceive goals to be shared by institutions and themselves and the number of individual needs satisfied in the group (March and Simon, 1963). March and Simon suggest that the amount of competition in a group and its prestige shape institutional identification.

Finally, as people become more visible as members of an organization, they perceive the organization to be more attractive; thus, their identification with the organization and their desire to announce their support increase. Stern (1988) suggests that employees of a corporation represent their identification symbolically through use of the company's name as an emblem. Such totems serve to generate group identification, promote respect and admiration for the group, and provide a source of explanation for the qualities associated with the group. Cialdini and others (1976) analyzed the tendency for students on campus to "bask in reflected glory" when their team wins by wearing school-identifying apparel after victories—and not wearing it after defeats (Wann and Branscombe, 1990). People associated with the University of Chicago take great pride in touting the number of Nobel Prizes, seventy-five as of 2003, won by people in the university community. They do not fail to mention that this feat ranks Chicago first among U.S. colleges and universities and second in the world only to Cambridge (Sanderson, 2001).

The essence of institutional identification then is that people want to announce and strengthen their affiliations with given institutions because they perceive themselves to be psychologically intertwined with the institution's fate over time. In effect, through the symbols, language, narratives, and practices that make them tangible, they come to relate with the values, norms, and beliefs of institutions—its institutional culture put to use. Consider the improved attitude of the extended college community at Tusculum related to the symbolic acts of planting flowers and repainting buildings. Institutional culture is what allows a person to personally experience successes and failures, which has the effect of deepening support.

Benefiting from Institutional Identification

The crux of institutional identification, therefore, is that when a compelling institutional culture enables people to appreciate what an organization is doing as attractive and when they believe outsiders view the organization in the same way, their identification with that organization is stronger. Naturally, organizations work to articulate what is distinctive, central, and enduring about themselves through a variety of cultural forms that reflect the substance of their institutional culture (Dutton, Dukerich, and Harquail, 1994; Dutton and Dukerich, 1991). Individuals with the intense institutional identification that a dynamic institutional culture produces are more apt to seek more contact with the organization, to cooperate with other members of the organization, to direct competitive behavior toward outsiders, and to be more active and loyal relative to the organization.

These are exactly the goals of people working in student affairs, academic and administrative units, and external relations at colleges and universities, a desirable end anywhere in any organization. To garner support for what they do, whether in the form of legislative appropriations, major private gifts, annual fund donations, applications for admission, or tuition payments, institutions must reinforce the notion that what they are doing is distinctive, central, and enduring. The same is true of building identification in the campus community for students, faculty, administrators, and staff.

Strengthening institutional identification is thus the key to institutional effectiveness (Martin and Epitropaki, 2001). Bartel (2001) connects strong identification with higher interpersonal cooperation in organizations. And identification can be an alternative to pay-for-performance human resource models by encouraging such positives as information sharing (Alles and Datar, 2002). Fiol (2002) notes that strong institutional identification can bind people together behind organizational change. (She suggests, however, that it can also limit the possibilities for organizational change by potentially blocking the view of new possibilities.) Chreim (2002) goes so far as to suggest that significant efforts at organizational change bring a shift in identification—*dis*identification and *re*identification stages for organizational members.

Identification is so important in higher education management because the two organizational images—perceived organizational identity and construed external image—fundamentally shape how people will behave. Identification is a powerful concept for those seeking to shape organizations and institutions (Albert, Ashforth, and Dutton, 2000; Brickson, 2000b). When images of an institution are positive, supporters are more likely to contribute to its life. Institutional culture can be celebratory in nature and provide these positive images, affording excuses for individuals, including external constituents, to become involved in institutional life in an intense and enduring way. And because repeated and meaningful contact enhances identification with institutions, the institutions are thus inevitably stronger when people—students, engaged employees, or active alumni—are involved.

The essence of management is to connect the goals of the institution and the goals of the individuals associated with it. Their overarching goal is to have people feel proud to be associated with an institution that is thought to have characteristics valued by others. A strong institutional culture allows just this feeling, encouraging people to engage with institutions by encapsulating what causes people to want to identify with them. And with this feeling comes a stronger campus community for students; an enhanced commitment from faculty, administrators, and staff who are increasingly asked to do more with less; and an increased willingness by external constituents to provide tangible support in the form of tuition, donations, and appropriations (Toma, 2003).

Nonprofit colleges and universities rely on a community of support, which consists of, among others, families who enroll their children, trustees who lead the institution and advocate for it, and alumni and donors whose contributions defray the costs associated with present and future operations. The foundation of this support can, to a great degree, be traced right back to the identification engendered by the organization's culture. People are more likely to support social institutions whose purposes and values are aligned with their own. When a person canvassing door to door in your neighborhood asks you for a donation, your inclination to give depends on an assessment of the importance and legitimacy of the cause. It is the same calculation the prospective Tusculum trustee had to make. His response was, like yours will be, influenced by previous knowledge of the organization or the ability of the representative to convey its purpose and importance. If the values of the organization conflict with your own, however, clever marketing and persuasive rhetoric are worthless.

In fact, each of us is a veritable prodigy when it comes to assessing values. We immediately sense the difference between a staid organization like the Sierra Club and the more gritty and controversial Greenpeace. Both organizations exist to preserve the environment. But the beliefs of those within the organizations about why the environment is suffering and their definition of reasonable tactics for achieving their goal are sharply divergent. Each organization's values appeal to distinct subsets of people. Extensive and prolonged contact with a particular organization—an environmental group, a house of worship, a political party, a higher educational institution—has the capacity to produce a truly profound sense of personal identification, particularly when people come to feel that their lives have been enriched and enlarged through the association. Such deep commitment is most likely when people view the institution as distinctive, central, and enduring and when the organization's purpose is to positively influence people's lives (Dutton, Dukerich, and Harquail, 1994). It is certainly an apt description of many colleges and universities. What makes the institution seem distinctive or special are the norms, values, and beliefs that guide people's behavior—the institution's culture.

Using Culture to Build Brand Equity

CLOSELY CONNECTED WITH institutional identification is conveying and building an institution's image as a brand. Like fostering strong culture to enhance identification, institutions develop brands with tangible ends in mind. They gain considerable advantages in doing so, building the intangible—yet measurable and certainly important—equity that comes with a strong brand. Once again, institutional culture provides a means to represent and make accessible what is accepted and what matters at an institution. In doing so, institutional culture, in both substance and form, highlights a university or college's appealing attributes that drive institutional identification. In much the same way, a robust culture provides the foundation needed to build a name brand, making the image of the institution apparent in appealing ways that people, notably those outside the immediate university community, can readily understand and are inclined to appreciate. These individuals include those who provide institutions with essential financial support, so conveying the right overall image, the institution's brand, is another critical example of institutional culture in the service of strategy and effectiveness in higher education.

Building a brand is essentially a matter of shaping a distinctive identity and projecting a coherent and consistent set of images to the public (Keller, 2003; Van Auken, 2003; Nilson, 2003; Aaker and Joachimsthaler, 2000). Acquiring, maintaining, and enhancing equity in a brand—the value that results from it—require strategy and execution. Like businesses, colleges and universities must work hard and smart to build themselves as brands. They must associate who they are and what they do with what people perceive to be positive and thus are interested in supporting. Indeed, the strategic management of brands is an important topic in the brand equity research literature (Myers, 2003; Campbell, 2002; Wood, 2000).

Sevier (1998) identifies institutional image as the most important resource in student recruiting and fundraising, arguing for the use of segmentation in marketing and engaging in marketing only after rigorous planning. Similarly, Keller (2003) adds that branding is a product of knowing target markets and the nature of competition within them, identifying points of parity and points of difference. By building their brand through marketing and other means, institutions attempt to link themselves with what people take pride in, what they value as a society, and what they identity with. In other words, institutions underscore what they consider to be distinctive, central, and enduring, appealing to the trigger for institutional identification (Dutton, Dukerich, and Harquail, 1994).

Institutions as Brands

Aaker (1991) defines brands as the names and symbols that identify the goods of one seller and differentiate them from those of another seller. Stein (1990) defines the concept as the "aggregate or sum of the feelings, beliefs, attitudes, impressions, thoughts, perceptions, ideas, recollections, conclusions, and mindsets people have of an institution" (p. xx). These perceptions are the ones that different key groups of people develop over time about particular characteristics and attributes related to an institution (Alfred and Horowitz, 1990; Alfred and Weissman, 1988). Keller (2003) suggests that organizations build brand and thus brand equity based on memorability, meaningfulness, transferability, adaptability, and predictability. A broad organization may include several brands, what is termed "brand extension" into a family of brands (Petromilli, Morrison, and Million, 2002; Randall, Ulrich, and Reibstein, 1998). For instance, the University of Michigan has a broad brand name associated with teaching and research at the institution but also has brands connected with its medical center, its sports teams, and so on.

Organizations and institutions create a certain mystique by focusing on special advantages so that their brand will be remembered when needed (Aaker and Joachimsthaler, 2000; Aaker, 1996; Arnold, 1992). Like the best-regarded firms, the leading universities and colleges engage in practices that cause them to "rise above the rest in prestige, status, and fame because they prize, pursue, and achieve uniqueness. They do so by developing management practices that reinforce their uniqueness and foster consistent images of the company as credible, reliable, responsive, and trustworthy. . . . The best-regarded companies love to proclaim their uniqueness. They actively rate themselves against a prominent peer group of rivals. They also practice assiduously some relatively mundane routines that help their products and services stand out, even in crowded and competitive industries" (Fombrun, 1996, pp. 23–24). These characteristics are, of course, the same ones linked with a strong organizational culture. Accordingly, a rich organizational culture is perhaps the key marker of the most highly regarded firms (Collins, 2001; Collins and Porras, 1996).

We would broaden Fombrun's argument to say also that it is not only "leading universities" but also successful institutions of all kinds that are adept at asserting a distinctive image. A large research university might focus on the number of notable faculty members (Chicago's Nobel Prize winners, for example), a small liberal arts colleges might trumpet the Pulitzer Prize–winning faculty member whom students can get to know in a small seminar, and a small regional institution may focus on its ties to the community. Tusculum moved from being "that Yankee school" (because it did a great deal of recruiting in New Jersey) and "in Greeneville but not of Greeneville" to being seen as a local asset under the leadership of the new president, who worked with the faculty to assert a compelling institutional image around the civic arts in the curriculum, enhanced the recruitment and enrollment of local students, and started a football team to boost enrollment and provide entertainment for locals in a football-crazy town. He also, of course, cultivated a relationship with the editor of the local paper and sought out local business leaders for the board, building on this new image. The renewed institutional culture at Tusculum was important in making the new image credible and was thus an important aspect of the institution's developing name brand. As Fombrun suggested was indicative of the strongest brands, Tusculum was well on the way to achieving distinctiveness and proclaiming and reinforcing it through a consistent set of images that would stand out in a crowded marketplace.

Although a clear image is available to all institutions, certain names and symbols have a special mystique. In business, they might be Mercedes-Benz or Cadillac in the automobile industry or the Prudential rock or Citigroup umbrella in financial services. Names and symbols communicate quickly what the corporation wants people to know about them and their products through a mix of information and aura (Selame and Selame, 1988). In higher education, names like Harvard, Amherst, and Berkeley have a certain mystique in higher education as a result of their long traditions as market leaders, the perceived value that their degrees offer recipients in the marketplace, the resources they have available, and the attractiveness of their campus atmospheres.

People admire these strong brands and the qualities that they believe them to represent, and they want to acquire the attributes that the brand has to offer (Blackston, 1995). At a minimum, certain people want to buy a product (or attend or support a college or university) about which they have heard (Terkla and Pagano, 1993). When goods or services are similar in quality and price, status and reputation are often what determines what people will buy (Selame and Selame, 1988). All things being equal, people want to go with something that is proven. The value of the names and symbols that represent what is known and positive about a corporation or an institution is thus an asset. In fact, the replacement value of a strong brand—the Mercedes aura or the Harvard mystique—is likely worth well more than the tangible assets of the firm or institution. Indeed, almost always, a brand must be built slowly, adding symbols and strength as it goes on (Wee and Ming, 2003). Yale did not become Yale overnight; it took the right combination of timing, resources, leadership, and good fortune. Indeed, the strongest brands have great intangible value that cannot be easily replaced (Dyson, Farr, and Hollis, 1996).

Brand Equity

Brand equity—the value of a given brand—is the important concept for our purposes in exploring the uses of institutional culture in higher education. It is the combination of assets such as brand loyalty, brand awareness, perceived quality, and brand associations (Keller, 2003; Hoeffler and Keller, 2002; Kapferer, 2000; Supphellen, 2000; Yoo, Naveen, and Lee, 2000; Aaker, 1991).

Brand equity is connected with closely related and inherently nebulous notions such as image, identification, values, investment, reputation, status, and prestige. Despite the intangible nature of brand equity, the attributes that make it up can be and must be measured, the brand equity research literature argues (Abela, 2003; Keller, 2003; Washburn and Plank, 2002; Mackay, 2001; Schultz, 2000, 2002; Ambler, 1999; Franzen, 1999). And all of these assets are linked, to some degree, with institutional culture. Culture highlights what matters in an organization and how it goes about its business, both for those in the organization itself and those who are "buying" it.

These perceptions about institutions are important because people do not necessarily respond to reality in making choices. Instead, they often respond to perceptions that do not fully correlate with quality (Perrow, 1961). The University of Notre Dame has long been considered more prestigious than its academic programs probably merit because of its successful and appealing football program. (Although the academic programs have certainly come a long way toward catching up in recent years.) Once again, images do not occur overnight, and sometimes images lag behind reality (Sevier, 1994; Terkla and Pagano, 1993). Because these notions exist more in the minds (and hearts) of people than they do in reality, brand equity is much more intangible than tangible. Princeton will still be Princeton; even if there is a considerable decline in quality at the institution (which is unlikely, given the resources that the strength of the brand can attract), the institution's positive image will likely persist. Here culture and image are similar; both are more intangible than tangible and, when strong, are persistent.

Brand equity has clear use for institutions (Keller, 2003; Aaker, 1991), which we can describe in terms of Aaker's four-part model. Aaker's four features of brand equity—brand loyalty, brand awareness, perceived quality, and brand associations—provide value to customers and constituents, to firms and institutions. Customers of corporations (and constituents such as students in higher education) benefit from strong brands because they can interpret and process information, have confidence in the purchase decision, and be satisfied in their decision to purchase and use the brand. "Knowing that a piece of jewelry came from Tiffany can affect the experience of the person wearing it: The user can actually feel different" (Aaker, 1991, p. 16). The same is true of the cultural capital that comes from an Ivy League degree. When a student "buys" an institution, he or she also buys a set of strong positive associations with that institution that many people hold.

In business, *brand loyalty,* the first marker of brand equity, reduces marketing costs, provides leverage with suppliers, attracts new customers by creating awareness and reassurance, and provides time to respond to competitive threats. These same values extend to higher education. Alumni relations are built around loyalty to the alma mater. It is a key basis for success in such activities as fundraising appeals. Loyalty is also critical in providing institutions cover with key constituents during crises, such as with legislators during lean budget years. Strong connections between institutions and constituents pay dividends when institutions need "their people" to step up to the plate and support them. And, again, it is critical to note that institutional culture is what drives and enables these connections, another illustration of the uses of institutional culture.

Having a strong brand also helps to create *brand awareness.* Brand awareness provides an anchor to which other associations can be attached. These associations are a marker of familiarity and suggest that people like the brand. They are also a signal of substance and commitment. People select known brands over unknown brands because they perceive the known brand to be reliable, in business to stay, and of reasonable quality. Brand awareness is a key in successful relations with such external groups as potential donors and prospective students. In short, brand awareness signals that the brand is one to be considered. When Stanford or Chicago recruiters attend college admissions fairs, their jobs are made easier because people know something positive about the name brands they represent. Similarly, one reason to establish a football program at Tusculum is to build awareness of the institution-as-brand.

The third attribute associated with brand equity, *perceived quality,* provides consumers with a reason to buy a product. It allows for differentiation between and among products, positioning them within markets and setting premium prices. It also causes people to become interested in the brand and allows for the brand to be extended into other areas or activities. People are more likely to buy into a new type of program—such as executive education when it emerged several years ago—at Harvard or Kellogg (Northwestern) or Wharton

(Pennsylvania) because the quality of these business schools is generally perceived to be so strong. The analogy here is to a new flavor of an established food brand (Toma, 2003). Tusculum has a challenge in this area in establishing its new curriculum around the civic arts, needing to make a credible case for quality and not only distinctiveness. But if it does, the benefits that will accrue to the institution are considerable in terms of brand equity.

Brand associations, finally, help people process and retrieve information about the brand, allowing them to differentiate between and among brands and understand the position of the brand relative to others (Dillon, Madden, Kimani, and Mukherjee, 2001). These associations give consumers a reason to purchase the product, create positive attitudes and feelings, and facilitate the extension of the brand into other areas. Those interested in Tusculum can associate the college with other liberal arts institutions but can use the new curriculum to differentiate between Tusculum and other campuses.

Developing and maintaining brand equity is of critical importance at higher education institutions. If a dynamic institutional culture has tangible uses, they, along with institutional identification, will occur here. Just as business firms benefit from brand equity because customers benefit, institutions benefit because students and other key constituents benefit. With strong brand equity, marketing programs are more efficient and effective, prices and margins are higher, revenues are more stable, opportunities to extend the brand are enhanced, there is more leverage in distribution and other trade relationships, it is easier to recruit top people, and there is less risk when crises occur (Keller, 2003). Strong brands provide an overall competitive advantage in a marketplace, even discouraging competitors from entering a given market. In essence, organizations, including higher education institutions, can use a favorable image with salient publics to control their dependency on the environment (Perrow, 1961).

Quite simply, having a good image makes institutional life easier. In industry, it allows salespeople easier access to audiences and greater self-assurance once there, like the 3M salesman cited earlier (Dutton, Dukerich, and Harquail, 1994). In higher education, those charged with external relations have the same advantages; consider the difference in the president's pitch to the prospective Tusculum board member between the first and second vignettes.

Prestige is also transferred to workers in professional and social settings, which can translate into improved morale and productivity (again, the link with institutional identification). Institutional stature also has "business" value. For instance, although all are treated equally in competition for projects or grants, the most respected organizations usually have an advantage (Garbett, 1988). In short, reputation widens options and reduces risk for firms and institutions (Cravens, Oliver, and Ramamoorti, 2003; Parameswaran and Glowacka, 1995; Cobb-Walgren, Ruble, and Donthu, 1995).

Building Brand Equity

Once again, developing strategies to advance brand equity is not the same as actually achieving it. It is very difficult to underscore institutional advantages in ways that will resonate. One way is to identify benchmarks relative to competitors (Sevier, 1994). Outsiders can—in fact, must—validate claims of quality, as in the case of rankings and other indices (Perrow, 1961). In other words, messages must be realistic. Brand equity cannot simply be declared but must be earned over time. Nevertheless, although images must reflect reality, those involved in external relations can select and promote those characteristics, perhaps through special events, that harmonize with key organizational and institutional goals (Garbett, 1988). For institutions that pride themselves on applied research and community involvement, achieving brand equity means running successful programs in their immediate community or region. Whether it is agricultural outreach, school reform initiatives, or social service, these programs reflect both institutional competence and a willingness to engage in meaningful partnerships with the surrounding community (Toma, 2003). The same is true of the new civic arts curriculum at Tusculum. These programs provide a platform from which the institution can get its name out while attempting to attach something distinctive and valuable to it.

In higher education, strong brands are also linked to institutions having clear values that they articulate through a variety of forms. These institutions have distinctive identities—norms, values, and beliefs that they continually announce and reinforce through symbols, language, narratives, and practices. Alfred and Horowitz (1990) suggest that the most successful higher education institutions are those marked by product visibility; continuous assessment of performance; management of cost sensitivity; capacity for innovation; response to pressure; timely strategic decisions; distinctive products, services, and operations; community and environmental responsibility; demonstrated expertise in communications; strong persona and visibility of leader; financial durability and soundness; traditional prestige; and capacity to attract and hold talented staff. Such organizational traits are a product of the distinctive and dynamic culture that is the essential ingredient of brand equity and the institutional identification that draws constituents toward institutions in ways that cause them to be willing supporters of institutional aspirations.

Once again, brands do not just happen: organizations actively build and strengthen them. Among the six factors that control company image that Garbett (1988) suggests, four have to do with the active management of that image: the newsworthiness of the company and its activities, communications, time spent on image, and memory decay (what the public forgets about the company). (The other two factors are the reality of the company itself and how diversified the company is.) Advertising provides one means through which institutions can build their brands (Franzen, 1999). Organizations also have various options and tactics at their disposal—logos and symbols, characters, slogans, packaging—and can adopt multiple strategies such as highlighting product quality, pricing competitively, using indirect channels, and launching private labels (honors colleges within larger universities, for example) (Keller, 2003). Secondary associations are also available through cobranding, endorsers, or sporting events (Keller, 2003). But even advertising has become more challenging in a more competitive marketplace with increased consumer and media fragmentation (Kapferer, 2001).

In the end, advancing the value of the name brand of the institution, particularly as it enhances institutional identification, is the essence of institutional advancement and external relations in American higher education. The role of external relations staff is to shape the images that these varied constituents have of the institution toward a unified, positive view (Sevier, 1998). Different audiences have different relationships with and ideas about universities and colleges, thus making the consistency and cohesion that result from a strong brand even more important. At large universities, for instance, alumni view institutions differently from other taxpayers; annual fund contributors and major individual donors have different conceptions from others and each other; individual, corporate, and foundation donors all differ in their ideas of the university; state legislators and business leaders, community residents, and state taxpayers each have their opinions; and prospective students and high school guidance counselors have yet another set of images of the university (Toma, 2003). Similarly, students, faculty, administrators, and staff each understand their campus differently, and a seemingly endless variety of subgroups within each group have very different impressions of the institution. A student body, for instance, includes traditional students, nontraditional students, part-time students, and minority students, to name a few (Sevier, 1994; Hearn and Heydinger, 1985; Melchiori, 1990; Stein, 1990; Grace and Leslie, 1990; Rydell, 1989). And external constituents understand the institution differently from those with more daily involvement.

Even though these members of the extended university community inevitably have different interests and agendas, they can all relate to certain broad images and messages. Here is where institutional culture is useful: it makes institutions accessible and understandable for various constituents and underscores what is noteworthy and meaningful about a university or college. And institutional culture itself can become part of the brand, as was beginning to occur at Tusculum in the second vignette about a focused, collegial campus. The corporate culture of firms like Saturn, Southwest Airlines, or IKEA is well known to consumers and a significant aspect of the appeal of the brand. In the end, institutional culture both supports the overall image of an institution and becomes part of that image. It supports the sort of reputational endowment expressed in the term *brand equity.*

Although culture is difficult to shape, it is possible—perhaps more possible than shaping image in ways that resonate with intended audiences. Consider the challenge at Tusculum. The campus was able to change its norms, become more collegial, and take symbolic steps such as painting buildings relatively quickly. It remains to be seen whether prospective students and others will really buy the distinctiveness and quality of the new civic arts curriculum.

Finally, it is important to remember that images associated with an institution can be positive or negative (Faircloth, Capella, and Alford, 2001) and that these images are never in an organization's or institution's full control. The concept of branding depends on not every organization's having the strongest image: there must be leaders as well as those who are either attempting to catch up or staking out a different market. (Not all institutions aspire to the Harvard brand; some focus on the convenience of local students and develop their brands accordingly, while others concentrate on keeping their prices low.) So how does the institution get people to pay attention? How does it get across the right messages? How can the institution change already formed opinions about itself (Sevier, 1994)? How do institutions know who is hearing the messages they are sending? Indeed, the identity of institutions—or the identification of people with them—more often results by chance than by design (Franzen, 1999). Nevertheless, it is crucial that key constituents learn about the broad vision of a campus as well as the important and exciting things that are happening there, even if institutions are sometimes limited in their tools to reach these people.

Understanding Institutional Culture

BEFORE ADDRESSING THE institutional culture in substance and form, relating it to institutional identification and brand equity, we briefly define the concept, discuss the disciplinary foundations of the study of institutional culture, note some major conceptual frameworks related to the topic, and comment on current approaches to the study of culture. We then explore typologies of institutions in American higher education and conclude with a discussion of subcultures in higher education. Institutional culture, as a topic, is studied from several different assumptions and in several different ways. Further, it tends to assume a quite different general shape at different institutional types. The same is true of subcultures. Among faculty, for instance, whether grounded in constructs such as institutional type, disciplinary domains, or otherwise, different subgroups have different cultures. Our discussion of the foundations of institutional culture complements the 1988 monograph by Kuh and Whitt, updating references, where applicable, and providing the foundation for the more concrete treatment of the topic that follows in the next section.

Defining Institutional Culture

Kuh and Whitt (1988) describe institutional culture in higher education as "the collective, mutually supporting patterns of norms, values, practices, beliefs, and assumptions that guide the behavior of individuals and groups in an institution of higher education and provide a frame of reference within which to interpret the meaning of events and actions on and off campus" (pp. 12–13). Culture binds together the diverse elements of any organization into a whole. Culture is deeply embedded within an organization, distinctive to it, and enduring, thus providing identity and meaning for members (Kuh, Schuh, and Whitt, 1991). In addressing the question of what culture is (and what it is not), Martin (2002) suggests the difficulty of defining organizational culture and notes that definitions often bear little resemblance to how researchers actually study culture (Ogbonna and Harris, 1998). Gallagher (2003) suggests that culture is not what an organization says it wants in terms of products and policies; instead, it is the values and beliefs, style, and behaviors that an organization rewards.

Institutional culture is different from institutional climate, the latter focusing more on strategy—shared subjective experiences of organizational members that have consequences for functioning and effectiveness (Schneider, Bowen, Ehrhart, and Holcombe, 2000; Schein, 2000). Pettigrew (2000) characterizes the relationship between climate and culture in terms of sibling rivalry. Climate, he suggests, is strategic and concerned with measurement, while culture has deep psychology and etiology (how people learn the ropes). In other words, organizational commitment grounded in culture is emotionally driven, and the same notion based on climate is strategic in nature (Virtanen, 2000). And although Payne (2001) notes the difficulties attendant in differentiating between culture and climate, Schein underscores the importance of differentiating between the two. For our purposes in this monograph, we focus on organizational culture—the emotional part of organizational life— but relate it to organizational strategy in discussing the uses of culture in building community and enhancing external relations. We frame this discussion through the research literature on institutional identification and brand equity, rather than purely on organizational climate.

Institutional culture has been described both as the glue that binds an institution and the lens through which participants in institutional life interpret their world (Peterson and Spencer, 1990, 1993). It affords the meaning and context necessary for people to band together in coherent ways as well as the understanding needed for them to know why they are banding together. Institutional culture thus serves the functions of conveying identity, facilitating commitment, enhancing stability, guiding sense making, and defining authority

(Gioia and Thomas, 1996; Kuh and Whitt, 1988). Cameron and Quinn (1999) suggest that organizational culture can be measured along six dimensions within an organization: dominant characteristics, organizational leadership, management of employees, organizational glue, strategic emphases, and criteria for success.

People are more committed to organizations with strong cultures (Chan, 1997; Smart and St. John, 1996), and organizations that believe in something are the most effective (Lund, 2003; Jassawalla and Sashittal, 2002; Detert, Schroeder, and Mauriel, 2000; Cameron and Ettington, 1988; Deal and Kennedy, 1982). Ashby (1999) identifies ten features of a great organizational culture: an almost missionary zeal; a sense of pride, sincerity, and cooperation; an attitude of constructive discontent; a value-based mind-set and management style; an emphasis on creativity and innovation; a focus on building role models, not just leaders; a sense of high expectations and professional standards; fair, commensurate compensation and incentives; a habit of celebrating success; and an adherence to the golden rule. Toma (2003) links the strong institutional culture that coalesces around the collegiate ideal with the institutional identification and brand equity that enable institutions to attract the resources from external constituents that enables them to not only maintain but to build.

Flynn and Chatman (2001), however, argue that stronger cultures reduce innovation in organizations. Strong organizational culture can be oppressive, even akin to cults marked by devotion, charismatic leadership, and separation from community (Arnott, 2000). And Gallagher (2003) cautions that a good culture does not necessarily equal success for an organization.

Disciplinary Foundations and Conceptual Frameworks

The study of organizational culture has its intellectual roots in three disciplines: anthropology, sociology, and psychology (Martin, 2002; Ashkanasy, Wilderom, and Peterson, 2000; Schein, 1992; Alvesson and Berg, 1992; Sackmann, 1991; Kuh and Whitt, 1988; Cameron and Ettington, 1988; Ouchi and Wilkins, 1985). Anthropologists popularized the field in the late nineteenth century, joined by influential sociologists such as Emile Durkheim

(Altman and Baruch, 1998; Wright, 1994; Sackmann, 1991). Contributions from psychology have focused attention on the ways social groupings shape the behavior of individuals (Lakomski, 2001; Schneider, 2000; Van Buskirk and McGrath, 1999; Frank and Fahrbach, 1999; Alvesson and Berg, 1992; Sackmann, 1991; Kuh and Whitt, 1988).

Anthropologists study basic social units and assume a unitary, albeit complex, culture. For them, the unit is a culture; culture is a dependent variable. The guiding assumption is that each unit, though complex, is also unified through a distinctive pattern of language, symbols, and behaviors that draw the group together. Two major traditions of inquiry guide this work, the functionalist and the semiotic. The functionalist approach relies on the researcher to interpret patterns arising from observed organizational events and activities. The semiotic approach, stemming from the work of Clifford Geertz (1973), attempts to surface and articulate how group members define and make meaning of their world through symbols and ritual.

Sociologists tend to research larger social units than do anthropologists and usually assume the existence of subcultures. For them, a unit may have multiple cultures; culture is an independent variable. In other words, culture is a heterogeneous variable for those taking a sociological approach, not a monolithic entity (Butler and Earley, 2001; Goffee and Jones, 2001; Hofstede, 1998). Their research on larger social systems—cities rather than villages, for instance—also produced the first theoretical discussion of subcultures: the notion that a smaller group may function within a larger society but hold a distinct set of norms, values, and beliefs.

Psychologists inquire into culture as individuals mediate it (Sackmann, 1991; Cameron and Ettington, 1988; Kuh and Whitt, 1988; Van Maanen and Barley, 1985). Thompson and Luthans (1990), addressing organizational culture from a behavioral perspective, note that culture is learned by and transmitted to individuals through the patterns of behaviors of multiple agents. That is, individuals observe how people around them behave, and those seeking membership tend to replicate common behaviors, although each person has his or her own interpretation of group values and norms and may choose to act at variance with them. Because it is established by the actions of many autonomous individuals, culture is difficult to change.

Another way of viewing culture is in terms of functionalist and interpretive approaches. In functionalist approaches, culture is something that an organization *has;* in interpretive approaches, it is something that an organization *is* (Allaire and Firsirotu, 1984). Furthermore, interdisciplinary approaches to studying culture are both common and valuable, leading to a plethora of frameworks, methodologies, and assumptions (Frost, Moore, Louis, and Lundberg, 1985). For instance, Tierney (1989) introduces critical theory as a dimension, dividing the means of interpreting culture in organizations into functional (all can understand culture and in the same ways) and critical (culture is not an absolute, and people interpret it in their own ways). In the functional approach, culture is thought to be cognitive and understandable. Functionalists believe that culture has manifest meaning and that all in an organization interpret it similarly. It is thus possible to codify abstract realities, and researchers can predict institutional culture. The critical approach assumes the opposite of each point. Culture is not necessarily understandable to either organizational participants or researchers, construction of meaning does not imply that all individuals interpret reality similarly, it is not possible to codify abstract realities, and culture is something to be interpreted and not predicted. Feldman (1999) also focuses on power relationships in organizational cultures by drawing on critical theory, and Ogbor (2001) discusses corporate culture as corporate hegemony.

Among other conceptual frameworks, Cameron and Ettington (1988) suggest that the study of organizational culture can be grouped into three categories. The first is social interpretation, which focuses on schema, meanings, and frames of reference as indicators and components of culture. The second concentrates on behavior, specifically patterns of interaction or activities that define shared organizational behavior. The third category is organizational adaptation, which centers on habituated solutions to commonly encountered organizational problems. Martin (1992) also categorizes the study of organizational culture into three perspectives. The integration approach focuses on consensus, consistency, and clarity in organizations. The differentiation approach concentrates on these same factors in subcultures, some of which conflict with each other. The fragmentation approach focuses on ambiguity in organizations where consensus, consistency, and clarity are as likely as the opposite of each. Martin (2002) argues that research on organizational culture usually takes a single perspective but that it is better to view culture from all three approaches (although doing so requires that the researcher abandon any notion of objectivity in his or her work).

Turning to method, Martin (2002) explores the links among studying organizational culture, qualitative research, and interpretive frameworks (Davey and Symon, 2001; Sackmann, 2001; Heracleous, 2001). She suggests that epistemological, methodological, and theoretical issues in research on organizational culture can be polarizing, as with questions about whether work should be objective or subjective in nature, whether researchers should be outsiders or insiders, whether generalizations are possible and desirable or the study of culture is inherently context specific, whether cultural research should be broad or narrow in focus, and whether depth of interpretation is the marker of quality or whether it can be sacrificed to increase the numbers of cultures studied. Martin also details practical and political influences on work addressing institutional culture, arguing that decisions on methodological and theoretical approaches inherently incorporate tacit or explicit assumptions about power. For instance, studies seeking to be value neutral often minimize or ignore normative differences. In the end, choices in method and theory create blind spots—contexts never studied and questions never asked.

Others focus on quantitative traditions in research on organizational culture (Payne, 2001; Sparrow, 2001) and even how economists study culture (Hermalin, 2001). Ashkanasy, Broadfoot, and Flakus (2000) and Cooke and Szumal (2000) explore the uses of questionnaires in measuring culture, while others focus on the relationship between culture and organizational performance (Wiley and Brooks, 2000; Wilderom, Glunk, and Maslowski, 2000; Kilduff and Corley, 2000).

Foundational Work and Contemporary Approaches

Although the study of organizational culture can be traced to the University of Chicago in the 1930s (Trice and Beyer, 1993), it did not come into vogue as a sustained area of study until the late 1970s and early 1980s (Alvesson and

Berg, 1992; Sackmann, 1991), when economic turbulence and structural changes prompted interest in Japanese management styles (Schein, 1992; Tierney, 1988; Wilkins, 1983). Frost (1985) suggests that more affective elements of the workplace, typically misunderstood or not recognized by corporate leaders, also fueled the rise in studies of organizational culture during the 1970s and 1980s. These elements include concerns about balance between life and work, changing concepts of success, and desires for community and other nonmonetary rewards from work.

Clark (1970, 1972) was an early, lone voice applying the nascent theories of organizational culture to higher education. His early work, such as his discussion of the nature of "distinctive colleges" (1972), emphasizes the capacity of culture to influence those inside and outside the organization. His exploration of the organizational saga (1972) explains a key factor in the formation of an organization's cultural identity. Clark observed that institutions form myths or stories that chronicle their moments of hardship and triumph. This "saga" reinforces the "collective understanding of unique accomplishment in a formally established group" (1972, p. 500). Clark argued that such shared understandings establish an organizational self-conception, which he argues is a major influence in institutional decision making.

Until the late 1980s, a paucity of work linked institutional culture to higher education. In 1988, two publications provided the conceptual foundation on which subsequent explorations of culture in higher education would rest. Kuh and Whitt's *The Invisible Tapestry* defined the various elements of culture and applied them to colleges and universities. Tierney's article, "Organizational Culture in Higher Education," examined the relationship between organizational effectiveness and "strong, congruent cultures" (1988, p. 7). Tierney noted, with some irony, that American academic institutions, though vastly understudied, embodied many of the characteristics of the Japanese firms being lauded in the business literature. Both kinds of institutions valued knowledge production (or problem solving) over the maintenance of rigid hierarchy. Tierney also pointed out that studies of academic management had focused almost exclusively on operational issues such as strategic planning and marketing. He then laid out a framework for cultural study in higher education, identifying six areas as central to any study of culture at a college or university: environment, mission, socialization, information, strategy, and leadership.

Recent work on organizational culture has focused on contemporary issues in organizational life, including the influences of technology, cyberspace, telecommuting, and freelancing (Lewis, 2002; Baumard and Starbuck, 2001; McKnight and Webster, 2001; Dunbar and Garud, 2001; Hedberg and Maravelias, 2001; Tyrrell, 2000; Bluedorn, 2000). Furthermore, research on organizational culture is frequently and increasingly cross-national (Cooper, Cartwright, and Earley, 2001; Ashkanasy, Wilderom, and Peterson, 2000). Sackmann (1997) notes the influence of national, industrial, organizational, and suborganizational cultures, saying that ethnicity cuts across organizational culture (Sun, 2002). Organizational culture is more pluralistic, diverse, paradoxical, and contradictory than often thought; thus, a cross-cultural perspective is warranted in its study. Parker (2000) agrees, suggesting the study of organizational culture must also include the state and society of which the organization is part, and Ashby (1999) notes that organizational culture has both micro and macro aspects.

Writing on organizational culture occurs in academic journals and scholarly books but also in the popular press and "how to" books, the latter claiming that understanding, harnessing, and eventually changing corporate culture provides the key to success in difficult economic times. Indeed, organizational culture has been trumpeted as a panacea for a wide array of organizational needs and ills (Parker, 2000; Trice and Beyer, 1993; Alvesson and Berg, 1992; Deshpande and Parasuaraman, 1986; Peters and Waterman, 1982; Ouchi, 1982; Deal and Kennedy, 1982). The popularity of writing on culture can be attributed to both the appeal and limitations of more comprehensive "scientific" and rational explanations for organizational behavior to both scholars and managers alike (Trice and Beyer, 1993).

Exploring institutional culture not only involves questions of whom to study—thus potentially excluding some—but also of what to study. The mission of the institution, as defined, articulated, and used on campus, and its history are central to understanding institutional culture. The convictions and influence of founders or influential leaders may be central to the ways in which members of an institution continue to view the institution's fundamental purposes

(Clark, 1972). In *Involving Colleges* (1991), Kuh, Schuh, and Whitt suggest that if one is to better understand campus culture at Mount Holyoke and Berea, it is necessary to appreciate the founding mission of each institution to provide education for poorer students. The same is true of the traditional importance of agriculture in institutional culture at UC–Davis and Iowa State, the connections with a specific municipality at Wichita State and Wayne State, the significance of football at Nebraska and Texas A&M—and republican values at Tusculum.

How people interact with the various environments at higher education institutions where they study and work is also important in understanding institutional culture. These interactions are influenced by such factors as location (is the campus in the country and isolated or in the city and surrounded?), physical settings (does the campus have places where people can interact?), and psychological properties (can someone be anonymous on the campus?). The status of current leaders, their styles, and the expectations that people have of them are telling in studying culture. Other key aspects of institutional culture are how people are socialized into organizations, what constitutes information in an organization and how it is disseminated, and how decisions are made at the institution and who makes them (Kuh, 1993a; Tierney, 1988; Kuh and Whitt, 1988; Masland, 1982, 1985). It is equally important to recognize the influence of external factors and external constituents in shaping institutional culture and to view these factors and groups as holistic and mutually shaping (Kuh and Whitt, 1988). As Chaffee and Tierney (1988) suggest, organizations are influenced both by external factors, including demographic, economic, or political conditions, and internal forces such as values, traditions, processes, and goals based in the history of the organization.

Institution Types and Institutional Culture

It is important to underscore that institutional culture is not monolithic. Values tend to differ across institutional types. Those at liberal arts colleges prize contact between students and faculty and believe that institutional policies should uphold this value through small classes, the extensive use of seminars, the maintenance of office hours, and so on. Indeed, it is a value common to many such institutions as exemplified in President James A. Garfield's reflection on his undergraduate years at Williams—that his ideal college consisted of Mark Hopkins, famed "prexi" and professor of philosophy, "on one end of a log and a student on the other." Similarly, certain values tend to be consistent among research universities—faculty should shape the curriculum, tenure is needed to preserve faculty rights, research is the paramount role of faculty, for example. Institutions that emphasize access or convenience for students, such as community colleges and the for-profit sector, also share common norms, values, and beliefs: curricular decisions can be made by administrators and courses taught by adjunct faculty, programs should remain flexible to respond to market demand, facilities should be convenient for students, and, more often than not, utilitarian and pragmatic design trumps aesthetic value.

Some have looked beyond the disparate norms and values of various institutional types in offering typologies of institutional culture. Cameron and Ettington (1988) propose such a typology: some institutions prize flexibility, individuality, and spontaneity (Apple Computers in the 1980s), while others stress stability, control, and predictability (IBM in the 1970s). They, along with Cameron and Quinn (1999), divide organizations into four types based on these two sets of variables (flexibility versus stability and external versus internal orientation): clan (flexible and internal), adhocracy (flexible and external), hierarchy (stable and internal), and market (stable and external). Each organizational type has a different "glue" that binds it together: types of leaders, measures of success, management styles, and so on. Clan cultures are based in loyalty and commitment to a strong leader and are focused on developing cohesion through teamwork, consensus, and participation (Chan, 1997). Adhocracy cultures are bound by a commitment to innovation, leading to cutting edge outputs, and are led by entrepreneurs under a management style that encourages individual initiative, freedom, and uniqueness. Hierarchy cultures are governed by formal procedures and policies and value longevity, predictability, efficiency, and stability. Market cultures concentrate on achieving goals under aggressive and competitive leaders who measure success by gaining advantage over peer institutions (Michael, 1997). Mason (2003) proposes that organizations are of three types: leader driven, plan driven, and evidence driven.

Birnbaum (1988) focused on institutional types with his four-part typology of dominant cultures: collegial, bureaucratic, political, and organized anarchy. And Bergquist (1992), drawing on Cohen and March (1974), offered a variant in describing the collegiate, managerial, developmental, or negotiating cultures at universities and colleges. Both underscore that although one culture may be dominant on a given campus, the other three are generally present to some degrees. In the developmental culture, for instance, Bergquist suggests that furthering the cognitive, behavioral, and affective maturation of its members is the basis of meaning at an institution. He aligns each culture with an "opposite" upon which it relies and with which it shares certain characteristics. The developmental culture, for example, arises from the weaknesses associated with the collegiate culture, with its stress on the work of faculty and faculty governance and tacit and untested assumptions about the dominance of rationality at the institution. Birnbaum describes his collegial culture as both enhancing and orthogonal: individuals both accept the overriding culture and hold values that are separate from the overall group but do not conflict with it (Martin and Siehl, 1983).

Those in the managerial culture derive identity and meaning from the structure of the organization, according to Bergquist. In the managerial culture, end results matter across the institution, and fiscal responsibility and effective supervision are prized attributes. Birnbaum frames this general type as the bureaucratic institution, with legitimized authority and formal structure as paramount values. In such an institution, deviation from the dominant culture is unlikely, as those interested in change simply depart (Perrow, 1970). In the negotiating culture, Bergquist contends that meaning resides in how politics determines the distribution of resources. It reacts to the shortcomings that faculty, in particular, view in the managerial culture but does not eliminate clarity in structure and authority. Birnbaum terms institutions based on competition for resources as political, where shifting alliances are the basis of institutional culture. Finally, he suggests that organized anarchy may be the model for the research university, with no single culture and only the broadest values (the continued viability of the institution, for example) of real importance. It does not rise to the level of a counterculture, however, as no direct challenge exists to the values of the dominant culture (Martin and Siehl, 1983).

These typologies build from early attempts to explain organizations focused solely on bureaucracy and structure. Weber (1947) argued that the modern bureaucratic organization is characterized by the division of labor based on skills and qualifications, hierarchical structures, rules of operation that are more or less stable and can be learned, and management that is trained to lead. Structural theories alone were found to be overly rigid and thus insufficient to describe how organizations really function (Bolman and Deal, 1997). Katz and Kahn (1966) argued that classic Weberian organizational theory neither properly accounted for the effect of organizational interaction with the external world nor allowed for anything beyond the dictates of organizational leaders in determining direction. Even Weber, in describing the legitimacy of authority, presages later theories of organizational culture. Although he concedes that authority can be based on legal grounds, he also asserts that tradition ("the way things are done") and the charisma of a particular leader also are important legitimizing factors (Weber, 1947). Indeed, more recent research on academic governance suggests that institutional decision making is far less linear—and even less rational—than earlier models asserted (Cohen and March, 1974).

Subcultures in Higher Education

Merton (1968) contends that any bureaucratic organization engenders subcultures within the broader culture (Birnbaum, 1988). Parker (2000) terms culture as "fragmented unities": sometimes members identify themselves as collective and sometimes as divided. Parker suggests that division in organizations is underplayed in organizational research. Subcultures are practically inevitable at colleges and universities, given the inherent differences in task and temperament among students, faculty, administrators, and staff (Ruscio, 1987).

Like institutional cultures, subcultures are grounded in norms, values, and beliefs. They emerge and develop in ways that the overall institutional culture does (Bolton and Kammeyer, 1972). Each is the product of persistent interactions between and among group members and provides the means through which newcomers internalize what matters to the group and how it operates.

Nevertheless, to be considered a subculture, the normative value system of the subgroup must only be distinguishable in some significant manner from the culture of the broader organization or institution (Bolton and Kammeyer, 1972). Schein (1992) suggests that subcultures develop when the overarching culture is weak and unstable, as when shared history is insufficient or shared experiences between and among subgroups is lacking. And it is important to remember that symbols in any organization may be illusory because they are not always universally shared (Morgan, 1996; Weick, 1995; Morgan, Frost, and Pondy, 1983).

Though a culture may be dominant, subcultures with distinct sets of beliefs and values can also be detected. Some form around one's role within the organization (the most obvious being students and faculty), though others may also form separate subcultures: administrators and deans, professional and technical staff, clerical and service staff, alumni and friends, local community and state legislators and bureaucrats. According to Clark Kerr, "Today, the large American university is . . . a series of communities and activities held together by a common name, a common governing board, and related purposes" (Kerr, 2001, p. 1). These subcultures relate differently to all aspects of university life, some perceiving themselves to have a more central place within particular customs, activities, and initiatives than others (Baldwin and Thelin, 1990; Trow, 1997).

Returning to our earlier example of the liberal arts college, quite different conceptions may be present within the institution, not necessarily about whether faculty-student contact is desirable but about how that contact should occur. People respond not to objective realities but to their own conceptions of what is happening (Neumann, 1995; Weick, 1995), and their positions in organizations often influence their perspectives. Faculty members may emphasize the pedagogical benefits of the arrangement, while students may appreciate more personal contact with the faculty and greater attention to their work; administrators may look on it as a cost of doing business or as an advantage in recruiting (admissions) or retaining (student affairs) students.

Some subgroups, however, may hold contradictory views. Borrowing from Gouldner's classic study (1957) of the liberal arts college, for example, "local" faculty—those who are interested in teaching and institutional matters—may embrace the idea of spending lots of time with students, both in and out of the classroom. "Cosmopolitan" faculty members, who want to conduct research and feel more invested in their disciplinary community, may see an emphasis on student engagement as problematic. Some may even oppose the dominant norm. For example, drawing on the Tusculum case, some faculty members may prefer to recycle old lectures instead of recalibrating them to incorporate the civic arts focus in the new curriculum. Similarly, some students might wish to remain blissfully anonymous in class, even at a place like Tusculum that is grounded in student participation.

Martin and Siehl (1983) describe these disparities between the norms of subgroups and the overarching culture in a simple three-part typology. The enhancing subculture accepts the overriding culture; an orthogonal subculture accepts the dominant culture but also holds distinct (though unconflicting) values particular to that group; and the counterculture presents a direct challenge to the dominant culture's core values.

Most research on subcultures in higher education focuses on either faculty or students. Given their centrality to the mission of higher education and the conditions attached to their jobs, faculty culture has received significant attention. And research on students, including student cultures, continues to dominate work focused on higher education.

Faculty work occurs within at least four cultures concurrently (Austin 1990): the academic profession, the academy as an organization, the discipline, and the institution type. Tierney and Rhoads (1993) generally concur, suggesting the presence of national, professional, disciplinary, and institutional cultures. Toma (1997) adds the presence of a culture shaped by the inquiry paradigm in which a faculty member works. As with any profession, the professoriat tends to draw particular kinds of people—ones whose values and sensibilities are broadly consonant with the academic culture and likely a certain segment of the national culture. The training process, including several years in graduate school, tends to reinforce these values, further informing them and acculturating faculty to the norms of academic life (Blau, 1973; Gaff and Wilson, 1971; Ruscio, 1987).

Along with an interest in a particular area of inquiry, arguably the most important values among the professoriat are creativity and autonomy—again, cultures of the academic profession and academy as an organization (Ruscio, 1987)—though beliefs and attitudes have been shown to vary according to discipline and mode of inquiry (Gaff and Wilson, 1971; Ruscio, 1987). When divided along four axes of study—humanities, social science, natural science, and professional—professors exhibit significant differences in attitudes, beliefs, practice, and lifestyle (Gaff and Wilson, 1971). Biglan (1973) classifies disciplines based on whether they are hard or soft, pure or applied, or life system or nonlife system. Becher and Trowler (2001) offer another approach to dividing the disciplines. Despite these differences, faculty subcultures that arise along disciplinary or inquiry lines most often fall into the enhancing or orthogonal type. They support the dominant purpose of the institution (mission), its norms, values, and beliefs (culture), and likely its significant aspirations (vision).

Students relate to their institution in a far less homogeneous way. Their subgroups sometimes form around extracurricular activities and social networks such as athletic teams, fraternities and sororities, and the marching band (Rhoads, 1995). These subgroups might also form along the lines of shared interests—everything from academic fields to particular music genres. Typologies of student cultures seek to differentiate between groups of students based on their interests and their relationship to the institution. Although these schema are a somewhat superficial means of discussing student values as they rely on generalizations, they are a useful way of illustrating some of the various ways students connect with their institution, sometimes holding values consonant with those of the institution (enhancing and orthogonal) and other times standing in stark opposition to it (countercultural).

Nearly four decades ago, Clark and Trow (1966) identified four student subcultures: collegiate, vocational, academic, and nonconformist. The collegiate culture is centered on the social trappings of college life such as football, fraternity and sorority life, and extracurricular pursuits. The vocational subculture sees education as a means to a career and college as primarily a credentialing way station—an observation subsequently made by others (Moffitt, 1991; Spitzberg and Thorndike, 1992). The academic subculture is most concerned with learning for its own sake. The noncomformists seek a "critical detachment" from their institution. Clark and Trow argue forcefully that each represents a distinct subculture, owing to the distinctive patterns of shared beliefs developed both by predisposition and by in-group socialization. They qualify the typology, however, by noting that no individual student is necessarily of one type but that, depending on the level of attachment to the college and their involvement with ideas, students move toward locating a comfortable peer group.

Horowitz (1987), in her history of collegiate life, points to three undergraduate cultures: the "college man," the outsider, and the rebel. Her findings underscore many of the same themes identified by Clark and Trow. Horowitz sees students as entering a world where they have no say as to the making or enforcing of rules. The student living the "college life" does so in moderated rebellion toward the academic culture established by faculty. This student values extracurricular life over academics, which are a nuisance and tolerated only to get grades good enough to pass. (Horowitz considers college life to be the dominant student culture.) The "outsider" freely buys into the academic culture but is an outsider to the prevailing undergraduate culture. The "rebel" openly flouts all campus codes, generally because he or she finds the faculty and institution lacking in academic quality and legitimate authority. Horowitz also notes the rise of the "new outsiders," a group that embraces academic work but is more concerned about getting good grades than learning.

Finally, Astin (1993) draws on annual surveys of first-year students to yield a more finely graded typology. He characterizes students as scholars, social activists, artists, hedonists, leaders, status strivers, and the uncommitted.

Institutional Culture in Substance and Form

O UR CONCEPTUALIZATION OF INSTITUTIONAL CULTURE—
as substance articulated through forms—has its roots in Geertz's semiotic approach (1973) to culture and the psychosocial interpretive framework of Thompson and Luthans (1990). Geertz focuses on symbols, language, and ritual. Thompson and Luthans frame culture as a seven-stage, personally mediated process. The middle stages, wherein multiple agents reinforce culture in multiple ways, are particularly important to how we conceptualize organizational culture. In addition, implicit in our approach to the topic of institutional culture is the existence of subcultures. Whether or not the subcultures are enhancing, orthogonal, or countercultural, as Martin and Siehl (1983) suggest, we contend that members of the various subcultures in an organization process the forms and substance of institutional culture in the same manner as the dominant culture, though not necessarily to the same ends.

We begin with a discussion of the substance of institutional culture in American higher education—the norms, values, and beliefs of universities and colleges generally and of individual institutions more particularly. We conclude by highlighting the cultural forms—the symbols, language, narratives, and practices—that make these norms, values, and beliefs tangible. Understanding culture allows an exploration of its uses, particularly the importance of strengthening institutional identification and building brand equity.

The Substance of Institutional Culture

Institutional culture comprises the shared beliefs, values, assumptions, and ideologies that bind a group together and provide a framework for group members to understand their setting. Institutional culture consists of the norms, values, and beliefs of organizational members (substance) and the more tangible ways that organizations express meanings (forms): literally, "the way we do things around here." Institutional culture thus has more subjective dimensions (shared assumptions, values, meanings, understandings, and so on) and more objective aspects (physical artifacts, organizational stories, heroes and heroines, rituals and ceremonies, et cetera), the former being less apparent than the symbols, language, narratives, and practices needed for conveying them (Duncan, 1989). Sackmann (1992) portrays these dimensions along three lines as holistic (ways of thinking, feeling, and reacting), variable (expressions of culture), and cognitive (beliefs, values, and norms). Kuh and Whitt (1988) term them "product" and "process."

According to Kuh and Hall (1993), the substance of a culture is the articulation of what constitutes acceptable behavior, the espoused and enacted ideals of an institution, and the tenets used to define roles and relationships (Thornbury, 2003; Srinivasan, 2003; Stackman, Pinder, and Conner, 2000). In short, the substance of institutional culture is common descriptions ("what exists"), common practices ("how things are done"), prescriptions for repair and improvement ("how things should be done"), and reasons and explanations given for an event ("why things are done the way they are") (Sackmann, 1991). Sackmann (1992) terms them dictionary knowledge (what is), directory knowledge (how things are done), recipe knowledge (what should or ought to be done), and axiomatic knowledge (the way things are done around here). Schein (1992) distinguishes between "espoused values" and "basic underlying assumptions," noting that the former is not always congruent with the latter. In other words, our ideals and our behavior are not always in perfect alignment, including at universities and colleges. For instance, in the first Tusculum vignette, students going home on Fridays did not conform to the ideal of the residential liberal arts institution. Nevertheless, Schein argues that those within an organization come to take such norms, values, and beliefs for granted, thus providing a shared framework for addressing all manner of problems of adaptation and integration (Schein, 1992).

Organizations in a given industry, or even types of organizations in an industry, may share general norms, values, and beliefs (Louis, 1983; Sackmann, 1992). Martin, Feldman, Hatch, and Sitkin (1983) note that even though organizations often claim to be unique, the stories they use to illustrate their distinctiveness tend to follow one of seven basic patterns. Their finding echoes Levi-Strauss's contention that a universal set of myths are individuated according to the needs of a specific culture. As a means of explaining the paradox of uniqueness, Kuh (1993b) writes that the ethos of an institution, not necessarily its culture, captures the special qualities that distinguish one college or university from others of a similar type. By ethos, Kuh means the moral character of an institution that imposes a unique coherence on collective experience reconciled by the institution's peculiar history, aspirations, and public image.

In higher education, the ideal of community is a common value and belief across traditional institutions—and one of the most prominent means of promoting a sense of institutional identification. It is also part of the brand of a place—its image, as understood particularly by external constituencies. This factor was what was so lacking at Tusculum in the first vignette, when students were not engaged in campus life, faculty were barely speaking with one another, and the local community had so little sense of the campus. Indeed, the concept of an academic *community* is ubiquitous in traditional higher education, although the concept is articulated differently at residential institutions and "commuter" institutions. As a norm, value, and belief, community embodies how things are done at American institutions, at least those, like Tusculum, who do not eschew it entirely for the pure convenience of students, as is the model in much of the for-profit sector. It short, community is "how things should be done." Because leading institutions of all types value strong communal bonds and active student life, this ideal is prized in American higher education. (It is also possible at all institutions, not just leading ones.) At residential institutions, the centrality of community in institutional culture thus confers an importance and a legitimacy on an institution and "the ways it does things" to audiences both internal and external (Toma, 2003). Even institutions that employ technology as a medium for teaching and learning have incorporated these same values expressed through Web-based cyber-learning communities.

Because organizational membership at universities and colleges is fluid—there are always new students and graduates, new hires, and recent departures and retirements—institutions must work at building the community that is so central to their the norms, values, and beliefs. From the moment a first-year student or new faculty or staff member arrives, the institution must convey the substance of its institutional culture (Major, 2000). For instance, orientation programs for new students attempt to impart what makes an institution distinctive, what gives it an identity, and what brings it together. Students memorize the words to school songs, learn campus legends and stories, and participate in initiation rituals and ceremonies. Such activities have the capacity to enhance an individual's sense of community and thus strengthen culture (because the relationship is circular). Students learn when they are more engaged, in relationships with others on campus, and through extracurricular activities (Evans, 1996; El-Khawas, 1996; Dey and Hurtado, 1994; Chickering and Reisser, 1993; Baird, 1988, 1993; Bowen, 1991; Bresler, 1989). Furthermore, a robust community is also central in the connections to an institution that cause former students to retain such strong attachments and become active alumni.

Building community involves the entire campus in embracing diversity, sharing leadership and responsibility, participating in campus activities, enhancing teamwork, focusing on internal communications, celebrating traditions, and articulating the values that mark a strong institutional culture (Gardner, 1989; Bresler, 1989; Kuh, 1991; Kuh, Schuh, and Whitt, 1991; Gilley and Hawkes, 1990). Such are among the uses of institutional culture. Notions such as community that represent institutional norms, values, and beliefs are not merely ends in themselves. They improve the lives of those in organizations and thus improve the lot of organizations themselves as connections strengthen and image clarifies, and support from both internal and external groups becomes even more firm and intense. Consider the more interactive relationship between the faculty and administration that emerged at Tusculum when the community was enhanced. The same is true of how it made attracting prospective trustees, and, one assumes, external support more generally, more plausible. They are the uses of institutional culture through strengthening institutional identification and building brand equity.

It is important to remember in considering the substance of institutional culture that different groups in institutions, particularly groups that have traditionally been marginalized, might not share all the elements of the dominant culture or perceive themselves to be fully integrated into the overall university community. Such groups might include commuter or part-time students on a residential campus or adjunct faculty. Moreover, some of the symbols, language, narratives, and practices through which norms, values, and beliefs assume a more tangible form for the general community may tend to exclude some groups. Martin (2002) suggests that researchers commonly focus on shared notions in defining organizational culture, thus underemphasizing subcultures and overemphasizing managerial and professional ranks. Toma (2003) suggests that spectator sports, which hold a central place in the expression of institutional culture at most large universities, may have this effect. In particular, organizational cultures can be gendered (Helms Mills and Mills, 2000; Itzin and Newman, 1995). Even though events such as a football Saturday would appear to be neutral, they are structured, at least somewhat, according to the symbolism of gender (Gherrardi, 1995). Fraternities and sororities are likely to have similar issues. Cultures can also be marked by race, (dis)ability, and sexual orientation, tending potentially to obscure the identity of an ever-increasing number of organizational members. Institutional culture, both in its substance and forms, can thus exclude when it is intended to include. So, unless the perspectives of various subgroups on the campus are considered, any analysis of the culture at an institution is incomplete, and the culture itself and the community that surrounds it are curtailed.

The Forms of Institutional Culture

How institutional culture takes form in a given institution is likely more peculiar to it than the substance of institutional culture. The broadest norms, values, and beliefs that make up the substance of institutional culture, like community, are usually characteristic of higher education institutions generally—or at least to a particular institutional type. It is also the case that certain cultural forms—symbols, language, narratives, and practices—may be common across institutions. Across academe, institutional culture takes form in the significant act of moving a mortarboard tassel from one side to the other at commencement. Having faculty line up in order of seniority at graduation or having representatives from other institutions line up by the year of their institution's founding are other value-laden cultural symbols common across institutions. Postings on office doors indicating safe zones for gay and lesbian students are tangible signals of norms, values, and beliefs held by individuals in the broader organizational culture associated with academe.

Still, the specific symbols, language, narratives, and practices used are typical as types—everyone has school colors, campus-specific jargon, founding sagas, for example—but these forms are unique to each university or college in how the institution operationalizes them (Deal and Kennedy, 1982, 1983). The following discussion explores how institutions give tangible form to the norms, values, and beliefs they hold, and whether these forms are those common to American higher education, to a particular type of institution, or to a given institution. These forms make institutional culture accessible, which is necessary in strengthening institutional identification through underscoring what is distinctive, central, and enduring about an institution, and in clarifying the institution's image in ways that build brand equity.

Trice and Beyer (1993) categorize cultural forms into four groups: symbols (objects, settings, performers); language (jargon, gestures, songs, humor, metaphors, proverbs); narratives (stories, legends, sagas, myths); and practices (rituals, taboos, rites, ceremonials). Pettigrew (1979) calls these forms "off-springs of the concept of culture" (p. 574; Sackmann, 1991); they, once again, transmit culture and meaning to individuals and groups. *Symbols,* the most basic and common unit of cultural expression, are something that stands for or suggests something else, like a logo or object that is meant to convey trust-worthiness or strength. *Language* is the combination of sets of symbols in infinite numbers of ways to convey many different meanings. *Narratives* use both language and symbols to express meaning in the forms of myths, sagas, legends, and stories. And *practices* such as rituals, rites, and ceremonials—the most complex cultural forms—combine all these forms to convey important cultural messages. Each group is explored in more detail below.

Symbols

Trice and Beyer (1993) define a symbol as something that stands for or suggests something else; a symbol takes the place of that which it represents, presenting a concrete indication of abstract values. According to Geertz (1972), symbols and symbolism help people give form to experiences and make sense of them. Symbols take the observer beneath the objective surface of organizational life into the underlying value structure and feelings inherent there, both positive and negative values and feelings (Geertz, 1972). In short, symbols represent what the organization means to participants and helps them sort through their experiences in the organization. Because they are so simple and straightforward, symbols pervade every aspect of organizational life. Symbols are revealed in the stories and myths, ceremonies and rituals, logos and colors, anecdotes and jokes that reach day-to-day life in any organization (Dandridge, Mitroff, and Joyce, 1980). Countless types of symbols exist, any one of which may also include multiple functions (Rafaeli and Worline, 2000; Peterson and Smith, 2000).

Accordingly, institutions and organizations commonly use symbolism quite consciously to "reveal or make comprehensible the unconscious feelings, images, and values that are inherent in the organization" through expressing their underlying character, ideology, or values system (Dandridge, Mitroff, and Joyce, 1980, p. 77). Symbols range from the most intangible representations of institutional characteristics—the indirect aspects that reflect the spirit and values of the place—to the physical artifacts that are the most concrete and immediately perceptible of all symbols (Gagliardi, 1990, 1996). These symbols have in common that they serve to connect people with institutions by evoking, signifying, and epitomizing them. Symbols provide a touchstone for people in the extended university community; they are a concrete representation of what the institution is and means. They provide tangible means for outsiders and insiders alike to appreciate the institution. Symbols are thus critical in both building campus community and enhancing external relations.

According to Dandridge (1983, 1985), symbols can be descriptive. For example, faculty and administrators dressed in academic regalia at convocation and commencement send the message that these events are of paramount significance in an academic community; through nonverbal cues alone, those attending receive the message that "this is important." Symbols can also be energy controlling, for example, attempts to inspire members or recapture feelings by giving an award or posting the dean's list or providing a specific forum within the organization for the acceptable venting of feelings. Alumni weekends and winter carnivals are energy-controlling symbols, respectively reminding alumni they are valued and allowing students to let off steam before final examinations. And symbols can be system maintaining, for example, campus architecture and landscaping that signals longevity, permanence, and exclusivity through ivy-covered walls, gothic architecture, and wrought iron fences and gates (Dandridge, 1983, 1985). Consider the symbolic significance of peeling paint and boarded-up buildings versus newly painted buildings and flowerbeds at Tusculum.

Symbols take the form of objects, settings, or performers. Objects become imbued with meanings as a result of their associations with particular institutions. A crucifix hung in every classroom is an important symbol in Catholic higher education, just as its removal signals a shift in an institution's norms, values, and beliefs. A logo like a university seal is such an object-as-symbol. The seal is likely to include icons associated with the essence of academe generally—suns, books, lamps, torches, or laurel boughs symbolizing knowledge and virtue, or towers and domes evoking power and prestige. Seals also include the institution's founding date, often in Roman numerals to suggest permanence, and sometimes include phrases written in Latin to suggest tradition and prestige.

Like the crucifix at a Catholic college, subtle changes in symbols may point toward much larger shifts in institutional values. Reuben (1996) notes that the original shield for Harvard College, adopted in 1643, featured the word *Veritas,* Latin for "truth," inscribed across three books. Shortly thereafter, however, Harvard devised a new shield. The motto, *In Christi Gloriam,* affirmed Harvard's primary mission as training ministers and underscored its role in maintaining the piety of a colony formed specifically to break away from dependence on the Crown and Church of England for spiritual direction. In the late nineteenth century, Harvard restored *Veritas* to the center of its shield, making it a visible symbol of the reforms that were transforming Harvard into a modern research university where students and faculty were absorbed in the task of discovering "truth."

The school mascot is another potent object-as-symbol that invites identification and clarifies image. At its most basic level, the use of such a symbol conveys membership in and an endorsement of the institution. Penn State University, both the main and branch campuses, use the Nittany lion logo, their mascot sitting majestically atop a mountain ledge, to underscore the strength and agility of the institution. Intercollegiate athletic programs use the mascot even more directly, attempting to evoke feelings of pride and success (Toma, 2003). As at Penn State, other areas of the institution may adopt symbols initially developed for another purpose (say, athletics). For instance, at the University of Michigan, the health system uses the maize-colored block M associated with the university's traditionally successful sports teams rather than the seal representing the academic side of the institution. Michigan, like other institutions, uses the M symbol to bask collectively in the success of a particular element of the institution.

A university's physical setting is itself a potent symbol. Institutions fortunate enough to have a signature building—"Old Main," the chapel, the bell tower—may use it in publications to convey distinctiveness or to suggest a proud tradition and enduring ideals. These structures often conform to the popular sense of what a university or college should look and feel like. These structures and landscapes symbolize what people aspire for or expect of their institutions (Toma, 2003). Institutions may use architecture to reinforce changes to mission. The College of New Jersey, for example, has remodeled the vintage 1960s buildings on campus to a classic Georgian look to underscore its evolution into a public liberal arts college (Toma and Morphew, 2001). In the 1990s, the University of Richmond added a host of new buildings with a college gothic look to reinforce its mission-driven ascendance to the ranks of selective institutions.

Finally, individuals may serve as important symbols. The president of the institution, imbued with symbolic value, is the "institutional icon" (Riesman, 1980). Members of the student body can serve such a purpose as well. It is a rare publication or Web page that does not feature groups of diverse students and others engaged in some collegial activity, whether reading in the library or tossing a Frisbee across a wide lawn. Intercollegiate athletes, mascots, cheerleaders, dance squads, marching bands, and flag corps are also performers whose purpose is to bolster school spirit.

These symbols and the substance of culture that they represent have concrete uses. They evoke the institution as both a concept and a concrete entity, making it more approachable, understandable, remarkable, and even esteemed to both insiders and outsiders. Symbols, as the most straightforward construct through which institutional culture takes form, encourage constituents to identify with institutions. They also make more tangible what differentiates the image of one institution from another and affords the strongest brands an equity that works to their greatest advantage. They also underscore the drivers of institutional identification, causing people to want to connect more fully with an institution. Once again, these ends are exactly those desired by people involved in student affairs, managing academic or administrative units, and external relations at higher education institutions.

Language

Language is the system of sounds, signs, and gestures people in any organization use to convey meanings to one another. Embedded in language are categories and rules that provide for more explicit meanings than symbols alone allow. Language allows for sets of symbols to be "combined in an infinite number of ways to convey many different meanings" (Trice and Beyer, 1993, p. 78). Language as a cultural form, according to Trice and Beyer, can be divided into several categories: metaphors; jargon and slang; gestures, signals, and signs; songs; humor, jokes, gossip, and rumor; and proverbs and slogans.

Jones (1996) suggests that norms are conveyed through a panoply of verbal expressions, including jargon, slang, memos, proverbs, traditional sayings, slogans, metaphors, pet phrases, nicknames for people and equipment, legends, cautionary tales, personal experience narratives, jokes, anecdotes, jests, beliefs, superstitions, rumors, rhymes, poetry, songs, ceremonial speech, and oratory. The activities through which norms are conveyed include play, recreation, games, practical jokes, initiation pranks, celebrations, festive events, parties, gestures, food sharing, rituals, rites of passage, staff meetings, retreats, ceremonies, architecture, interior design, quality of equipment, manuals, organizational charts, bulletin boards, posters, photos, memorabilia on display, costumes, company uniforms, standard attire, and decoration of offices or equipment (Trice, 1985; Trice and Beyer, 1984).

Such language has uses, allowing those associated with a campus community, including external constituents, to speak the same language, thus strengthening the bonds of association across various constituencies. Language also provides the means to express an institution's image—an image that becomes sharper as the means to express institutional culture strengthens.

One of the most powerful forms of language is the metaphor. Metaphors offer the opportunity to understand and experience one type of thing in terms of another type of thing: seeing something as though it is something else (Putnam, Phillips, and Chapman, 1996). Metaphors have "multiple interpretations and allow communication about things that are elusive and complicated, yet highly important. The essence of wine, for example, is captured or discussed through metaphors like 'impish, flaccid, accessible, and steely'" (Deal and Kennedy, 1983, p. 503). Metaphors bring complex structures to life for individuals (Putnam, Phillips, and Chapman, 1996; Pondy, 1983). It is usually easier to understand a particularly collegial institution as "a loving, if sometimes somewhat dysfunctional, family" or a more bureaucratic institution as "a well-oiled machine" (or one "held together with chewing gum and duct tape"). Such metaphors bring to life complex structures for people. They also describe a particular institution (or product or service) by likening it to a similar type (Putnam, Phillips, and Chapman, 1996). Moreover, metaphors can express several meanings at once. A familiar phrase on campuses when meetings start late is "We're on [insert the name of the institution] time." The phrase is used both affectionately, as a means of indicating that the institutional pace is more humane, and also somewhat derisively, but it also implies vexing institutional inefficiency.

Jargon and slang are other means of conveying a sense of belonging. Jargon is specialized language particular to an occupation or group. A faculty member knows what the terms "peer review" and "refereed articles" mean. On any American campuses, nicknames, shorthand, or initials commonly identify parts of campus, buildings, academic or administrative units, and even particular people. Hummon (1994) notes the relationship between slang and culture, a link noticed particularly in research about late-nineteenth and early-twentieth century students. He argues that slang has been used to describe virtually every facet of campus life. As student culture often stands, at least to some degree, in opposition to the faculty, slang therefore serves an important function of differentiating students from authority (Horowitz, 1987). Though slang is certainly a form of language and as such a significant ingredient in the cultural stew, it is not accepted as formal language. Use of slang is thus an expression of rebellion (Hummon, 1994). At the University of Georgia (as elsewhere) students have a particular slang: "ballin'" is feeling lucky, to be "beamed" is to be drunk, and a "bobblehead" is an annoying or irritating person. Some campuses even include in their guidebooks for incoming transition. What jargon and slang have in common is that they are initially inaccessible to newcomers and outsiders, but once they are learned, a person has demonstrated his or her desire for membership in an organization.

The same is true of gestures, signals, and signs on campus that have meaning only to people versed in the culture. A multitude of gestures, signals, and signs are represented at spectator sports: at the University of Texas, for instance, fans signal their support through the "Hook 'em Horns" hand gesture (Toma, 2003). Toma suggests that spectator sports are also central in the campus songs that contribute to institutional culture, making them both accessible and distinctive to insiders and outsiders alike. The same is true of campus glee clubs that keep the campus-specific songs alive that were once such an important part of campus life.

Campus-specific humor, jokes, gossip, and rumor can also convey the norms, values, and beliefs of an institution. Those at "State" or "A&M" are often teased by "University of" graduates as being unsophisticated and less concerned with academic excellence. "He didn't go to college; he went to State," the joke might go (Toma, 2003). The "State" and "A&M" people repay in kind by calling "University of" people elitist, with their heads in the clouds and note that State U. students know how to "work hard and play hard." In the Ivy League, the purpose of scramble bands at football games (their version of marching bands) is to make fun of the opposing campus or the community surrounding it. At Harvard's graduation, a senior gives a speech entirely in Latin to those assembled, and only the graduating class (who are provided with an English translation) laugh or cheer at appropriate times. Students at the

Massachusetts Institute of Technology are famed for their "hacks"—grand practical jokes that require tremendous ingenuity and élan, including the assembling of an entire automobile on a campus building roof and draping the entire MIT dome with a covering that made it look like the *Star Wars* droid, R2-D2. Certainly, gossip and rumor are present on any campus (as in any organization). Are budget cuts or program closures imminent? Who will be the next president or dean?

Proverbs and slogans are common at higher education institutions. Proverbs are short statements of folk wisdom; slogans are intentional statements. Most institutions have slogans that they use in advertising; their intention is to link them with institutional values to build the institution's image. Campuses are "hidden gems" or "public Ivies," or they are the largest employer in the state or county. Repeating that Tusculum is the oldest college in the state and the oldest Presbyterian coeducational institutional nationally serves this purpose. The same is true when locals call it "that Yankee college." Proverbs in higher education might focus on students' work ethic; for instance, State U. students often work hard and play hard or know how to party.

These proverbs and slogans may relate to the ideology common to campuses. Ideology is a system of beliefs about how the world operates and whether those systems are right or wrong, and it is a key attribute of the language and symbols that go into it. In organizations, ideology leads to broad, often moral diagnoses of situations and eventually to action (Pettigrew, 1979; Allaire and Firsirotu, 1984). Students at certain institutions, for instance, value professional training and practical courses more than knowledge for knowledge's sake and act accordingly in completing their academic work. Similarly, certain military or religious traditions shape ideology at certain institutions. The Corps of Cadets is central in the ideology that shapes the culture at Texas A&M, just as the religious beliefs and teachings of the Holy Cross order are at Notre Dame (Toma, 2003). The same is true of social and political sensibilities: conservative Pepperdine University is simply different from progressive Hampshire College.

The notion of ideology underscores that although cultural forms like language are common across institutions, the details associated with these forms are different at different places, and the intensity with which people embrace culture differs across campuses. Put another way, the words to the fight song may be different at different places, but there is still a fight song at each—although people may sing it more often and with more spirit at some schools. What is common is the use of collegiate forms to make institutions more accessible while representing them in tangible ways to broad and diverse audiences—which is what drives the institutional identification and brand equity that are the results of establishing and portraying a rich institutional culture.

Narratives

Narratives use language and symbols in the forms of myths, legends, sagas, and stories to help people make sense of their environments. Like symbols and language, narratives can transcend an institution's boundaries and become part of its image—its brand. These myths, sagas, legends, and stories related to and by people who seek association with the institution become an important part of its cultural fabric.

Myths are dramatic, vague, and unquestioned narratives of imagined events, usually used to explain the origins or transformation of something viewed as serious or sacred. George Gipp has taken on mythical stature at Notre Dame based on the mostly imagined story of him on his deathbed asking Coach Rockne to "win one for the Gipper" (Toma, 2003). The Gipp myth has come to represent a set of values—selflessness, determination, success—that those at the University of Notre Dame like to associate with themselves. At the University of Michigan, stepping on the M in the middle of "the Diag" will doom a student to failing his or her first bluebook examination, the statues of pumas in front of the Natural History Museum roar if a virgin walks past (they have never roared), and kissing someone under the Engineering Arch guarantees marriage to that person. The statue of Testudo the Terrapin at the University of Maryland is both symbol-as-object and symbol-in-action, as students are told that, when they walk past the statue, they should rub its nose (which has become quite shiny over the years) for good luck.

Sagas are like myths but are based on accounts of historic events usually framed in romantic terms. A saga is the collective understanding of a formally established group's accomplishments. Such an understanding provides a rational explanation of how certain means led to certain ends, but it also helps turn a formal place into a beloved institution (Clark, 1972, 1981). Institutional sagas facilitate loyalty to the organization in "believers," helping them to take pride in and identity from the organization. Sagas are rooted in history and vary in durability. They often revolve around founders or leaders at times of crisis or decay. The turnaround at Tusculum has the potential to someday be such a saga, and certainly its founding on republican ideals is that.

In short, sagas formalize or memorialize a sense of unity in an organization. "With deep emotional commitment, believers define themselves by their organizational affiliation, and in their bond to other believers they share an intense sense of the unique," Clark (1972) writes in describing the uses and impact of institutional sagas (p. 183). Loyalty causes people to stay with a system and work to improve it. It also reduces isolation and increases pride; to be effective, people need to understand where they have been and where they are going (Tierney, 1991). Tierney notes, however, that some wrongly view sagas as organizational realities that everyone can understand and that everyone similarly interprets them. He notes further that sagas often do not reflect concern with social justice. That said, founding documents of institutions and contemporary mission statements based on them are routinely idealistic.

At the University of Notre Dame, the story of Father Sorin's founding the school in the Indiana wilderness is a key element in the Notre Dame saga. The story of Father Sorin's accomplishments against great odds underscores the values of ingenuity and commitment to explain the rise of Notre Dame to national prominence as an institution. The same is true of Thomas Jefferson's effort to democratize higher education through the founding of the University of Virginia, Van Hise's Wisconsin Idea of public service to the state, or Rockefeller and Harper's vision for Chicago as a great research university. Once again, the power in these stories is that they are considered to say something about the values, norms, and beliefs of those associated with the institution.

Pacific Lutheran University was founded by a group of Lutherans who had traveled from the Midwest to the Pacific Northwest. From its founding, the institution has been on a tight budget (if not in outright financial peril.) An often told story, used as a cultural touchstone to elucidate this point, is of the college's first president's trekking to Alaska to join the late-nineteenth century gold rush but returning with only a set of moose antlers for his efforts. This story holds value in affirming the idea that students, faculty, and staff at the institution may at times be asked to make a special effort to help the institution but that they should not expect any get-rich-quick solution.

Legends are similar to myths and sagas except that they include some elements of heroics and wonder. At Syracuse, the number 44 has mythical status. All-American running back Jim Brown, often cited as the greatest football player ever, wore the number in the 1950s. Following Brown, Heisman Trophy winner Ernie Davis also wore number 44. His death from leukemia shortly after leaving Syracuse inspired Floyd Little, another All-American and number 44, to attend Syracuse. The number has transcended football at Syracuse to become a symbol for the university itself. The campus telephone exchange begins with 44, its zip code is 13244, and it is no surprise that a popular bar near campus is named "44s" (Toma, 2003).

Stories convey important cultural meanings (Smith and Keyton, 2001; Wilensky and Hansen, 2001; Gabriel, 2000; van Riel, 2000; Shaw, 2000; Larsen, 2000). They can even be used to reify collective efforts, as illustrated at Tusculum College. After a successful institutional transformation there, a number of accounts emerged marking moments in the institution's achievement. One describes three senior professors who had become so estranged that they had not spoken to one another in years (an amazing feat, given the relatively small size of the entire faculty). The new president sent the three to a conference on curriculum reform. That activity, and their subsequent collaborations on behalf of the change effort, repaired the rift among them. A wide range of institutional members used this story to underscore the institutional healing that occurred during the change effort (Hartley, 2002). Indeed, stories, like myths, sagas, and legends, are important indicators of values shared, understandings about how things are to be done, and the consequences of compliance or deviance. They facilitate memory, generate belief, and encourage commitment by appealing to legitimate values (Martin and Powers, 1983; Wilkins, 1983).

Practices

Activities in any organization, such as rituals, rites, and ceremonials, have instrumental purposes and are intended to convey important cultural messages to insiders and outsiders alike (Arens, 1976; Chaney, 1993; Kafka, 1983; Lundberg, 1990; Martin and Frost, 1990; Pace, 1962; Van Maanen and Barley, 1985). Rites and ceremonials are the most complex and elaborate cultural forms, connecting several other forms.

Rites are "dramatic, planned sets of activities carried out for the benefit of an audience" (Trice and Beyer, 1993, p. 80). One type of rite, the "secular ceremony," marks rites of passage into or within any organization; Manning (1993), building on the work of Van Gennep (1960), divides rites of passage into three stages—separation, transition, and incorporation. First-year student orientation is a common rite on American residential campus. Elements of fraternity or sorority rush have the same purpose. At Virginia Military Institute, upperclassmen challenge first-year students, called Rats, to prove themselves by physical exercise (usually push-ups) or by reciting portions of the Rat Bible, a collection of facts about the institute. And at many medical schools, the first donning of the white lab coat and switching from the short white coat to the long one upon becoming a resident are important rites.

Ceremonials are several rites connected in a single occasion (Schein, 1992). They are stylized and deliberate performances with a collective dimension that are repeated from time to time. They also include evocative style and staging intended to engage and focus the audience's attention (Moore and Myerhoff, 1977). Higher education is replete with ceremonies such as the inauguration of a new president.

Rituals are standardized, detailed sets of techniques and behaviors expressing common identities that tell people what they are supposed to do. (Taboos are the opposite of rituals and express behaviors that are socially undesirable and thus forbidden.) Rituals are formalized "dramas of persuasion"— staged and stylized versions of how things should be and beliefs about how things are that describe and shape cultural patterns. These events reinforce the traditional social ties between people by symbolizing the underlying social values upon which the social structure of a group rests (Geertz, 1973, p. 142). At Cornell, on Dragon Day each April, entry-level architecture students participate in the rite of building a papier-mâché dragon and marching across the engineering quad in anticipation of a designated engineering student's lighting it on fire. As several people watch, his or her fellow students then throw toilet paper on the fire to make it larger. Even the Rats at VMI have a ceremony, called "breakout," that marks their passage into being "true" first-year students by running down a muddy hill.

While symbols store meanings, as in a logo or an object, rituals dramatize them and myths relate them. And they do so in a way that "sums up, for those for whom they are resonant, what is known about the way the world is, the quality of the emotional life it supports, and the way one ought to behave while in it" (Geertz, 1973, p. 127). Cultural practices such as rituals are critical in institutional life because they keep ideology alive and establish and reinforce what is legitimate or unacceptable in an organizational culture (Pettigrew, 1979; Kamens, 1977). Rituals are more active than passive activities; people actually take part in them (Harris, 1983). In fact, it is their participatory quality that makes rituals different from drama (Gluckman and Gluckman, 1983).

Convocations and commencements are ubiquitous annual academic rituals rife with symbolism—the formal march into the hall, the wearing of academic regalia, speeches from the president and others, the awarding of honorary degrees, the reading of names of graduates, and so on. Convocation and commencement together operate as ritual bookends to the academic year, opening and closing a defined, communal period of teaching and learning. They are also cultural forms of entrance and exit from an academic community, the exit sealed with the credential of the earned degree. In fact, some institutions link the two ceremonies. The convocation ceremony at the University of Pennsylvania has first-year students march roughly the same route they will march four years later as seniors.

At convocation, faculty march in wearing academic regalia while students typically wear street clothes, identifying the students as neophytes in the community of learning. Commencement ceremonies see students join faculty in wearing formal academic robes, signifying that they have earned a place in a community of scholars. The events differ at institutions based on differences in institutional culture. Commencement at Cleveland State, for example, certainly takes on the culture of the institution. Whereas at many established and traditional schools, a graduation ceremony might be somewhat reserved or solemn, at Cleveland State it is a joyous affair. Raucous cheering and yelling typically greet the announcement of most graduates. This boisterous behavior signifies family and friends' joy in recognition of the graduates' achievement, for graduates, often first-generation college students, have often attended one or two classes at a time, all the while fulfilling family and job obligations (Dubrow, 2003).

At religious colleges, convocation and commencement rituals often include human and symbolic representatives of the faith. Priests or ministers might officiate, religious banners and other objects might be prominent in various elements of the events, and special prayers might be spoken. Religious colleges use convocation and commencement to manifest the bond between institution and faith, even if the bond has become largely symbolic and not pervasive in daily academic and social life (Dubrow, 2003).

So powerful are these cultural connections that those who explore the ritual aspects of institutional culture frequently liken it to a secular religion. Stein (1983) describes a Nebraska football game as people congregating to reenact their relationships to sacred objects and to reinforce their own values: it is not just a game but something closer to a ritualized civil religion. Like religion, a Cornhuskers game uses intricate rituals to place events in a traditional and worldly view in a setting that is not part of ordinary life or the profane world of everyday routines (Arens, 1976). As with religion, rituals in higher education enforce a community's commitment to its core values and provide controlled environments in which to express emotion. Both are a source of deep personal meaning and struggle to explore ultimate questions.

These rituals, reenacted annually, present and validate models of unity and success—models that are commonly thought to apply to other areas of institutional life (Montague and Morris, 1976). Ritual aspects of events encourage a sense of belonging and community in participants, similar to membership in a family (Stein, 1983). Institutions use such connections to advantage in external relations and other activities that seek to enhance the institutional identification needed to drive tangible support of the institution. Furthermore, rituals impart to a large group of participants the values that communities hold and to which they aspire. Accordingly, rituals can be important socializers of dominant cultural values, whether for the institution or the society, providing meaning and purpose to participants (Diamond, 1993).

These rituals, ceremonies, and rites are the most complex forms of the institutional culture that makes individual universities distinctive. They incorporate symbols, language, narratives, and other practices to give tangible form to the norms, values, and beliefs that an institution adopts and attempts to enhance. These norms, values, and beliefs are generally common across large institutions, centering on the community so closely associated with the collegiate ideal and the need to be recognized for academic and other efforts (Toma, 2003). It is the symbols, language, narrative, and practices associated with the institution that matter, making otherwise ordinary institutions distinctive. None of this is to suggest that the norms, values, and beliefs that large institutions hold—the substance of institutional culture there—do not matter. On the contrary, they connect people with institutional life through community and pride, a bond made more tangible and more resolute through the cultural forms that are unique to each institution.

Institutions use these ties and stress their distinctiveness when attempting to appeal to the important constituents that provide them the support that enables institutions to not only survive but also to thrive and build. In furthering community, institutional culture adds distinctiveness to otherwise similar large and impersonal institutions. These are the uses of institutional culture at universities and colleges. It is what builds identification among individuals associated with institutions and allows institutions to enjoy the benefits that come along with building a strong brand name.

Using Institutional Culture to Strengthen Institutional Identification and Build Brand Equity

IF INSTITUTIONAL IDENTIFICATION and brand equity are the keys to effective external relations, effective management, and rich campus community and they are the products of strong institutional culture, what can institutions realistically do to enhance institutional culture? How can they foster the shared ideals and values that provide the frame of reference for those symbols, language, narratives, and practices that people will come to associate with the institution? After all, it is the unique institutional culture that makes otherwise similar "products" in higher education distinctive and thus attractive to both internal and external audiences.

We regret to say that if developing, maintaining, and enhancing institutional culture were simple, all higher education institutions would enjoy a strong one. But it is not so simple. Schein (1992) suggests that "we all know of groups, organizations, and societies where cultural elements work at cross purposes with other elements, leading to situations full of conflict and ambiguity. This may result from insufficient stability of membership, insufficient shared history of experience, or the presence of many subgroups with different kinds of shared experiences. Ambiguity and conflict also result from the fact that each of us belongs to so many groups that what we bring to any given group is influenced by the assumptions that are appropriate to our other groups" (p. 5). Schein notes further that culture formation, by definition, strives toward patterning and integration, even though the experience of many groups is that a strong culture remains elusive. Harris and

Ogbonna (2002) discuss unintended consequences associated with attempting to manage culture, and Parker (2000) argues that culture cannot really be managed.

Recommending specific ways to strengthen institutional culture is outside the scope of this monograph. Instead, we refer readers to recent work on organizational change, much of which gets at the uses of institutional culture and suggests concrete approaches. Hartley (2002) suggests that one way for an institution to attempt to manage institutional culture is to clarify institutional purpose—the mission of the institution. Hartley writes about organizational change, a topic also explored by Kezar in this series in *Understanding and Facilitating Change in Higher Education in the 21st Century* (2001). In recent work, she and others have linked organizational culture and organizational change (Kezar and Eckel, 2002; Denison 2001; Lundberg, 2001; Nadler, Thies, and Nadler, 2001; Michela and Burke, 2000; Hatch; 2000; Zammuto, Gifford, and Goodman, 2000; Markus, 2000; Sathe and Davidson, 2000; Bate, Khan, and Pye, 2000; Eckel, Green, Hill, and Mallon, 1999). Finally, our work in this monograph builds from our own recent projects in which we explore institutional culture, particularly two books, *Football U.: Spectator Sports in the Life of the American University* (Toma, 2003) and *A Call to Purpose: Mission-Centered Change at Three Liberal Arts Colleges* (Hartley, 2002), and a dissertation, *It's Just the Way Things Are Done Here: The Role of Institutional Culture in the Process of General Education Curriculum Reform* (Dubrow, 2003).

A 2000 Kellogg Commission report focuses on strategies for restoring institutional cohesion in universities and colleges, arguing that it requires strong institutional culture. Campus culture is challenged, however, by institutions' becoming more complex and more comprehensiveness, and many cultures at many institutions (academic, student, administrative, athletic, for example) are only growing more disconnected. The report identifies the need for large institutions be rebalanced and reintegrated. Throughout our discussion, we provide the theoretical and conceptual bases institutions need to enhance their shared ideals and frames of reference as well as the symbols, language, narratives, and practices needed for conveying these ideals and frames. Institutions do not rebalance and reintegrate simply to do so.

Tangible ends and real uses come with the strong culture the Kellogg Commission report champions. The enhanced campus community and more effective external relations that come with strong culture and the institutional identification and brand equity that accompany it are exactly what drives the good will that enables healthier acquisition of resources. And it is what enables institutions to serve their ambition not only to maintain but also to expand.

References

Aaker, D. A. (1991). *Managing brand equity: Capitalizing on the value of a brand name.* New York: Free Press.

Aaker, D. A. (1996). *Building strong brands.* New York: Free Press.

Aaker, D. A., and Joachimsthaler, E. (2000). *Brand leadership: Building assets in an information economy.* New York: Free Press.

Abela, A. (2003, May). Additive versus inclusive approaches to measuring brand equity: Practical and ethical implications. *Journal of Brand Management, 10,* 342.

Adler, P. A., and Adler, P. (1988). Intense loyalty in organizations: A case study of college athletics. *Administrative Science Quarterly, 33,* 401–417.

Albert, S., Ashforth, B. E., and Dutton, J. E. (2000, January). Organizational identity and identification: Charting new waters and building new bridges. *Academy of Management Review, 25,* 13–17.

Albert, S., and Whetten, D. A. (1985). Organizational identity. In L. L. Cummings and B. M. Staw (Eds.), *Research in organizational behavior* (Vol. 7, pp. 263–295). Greenwich, CT: JAI Press.

Alfred, R. L., and Horowitz, M. (1990). Higher education and public perception: Dynamics of institutional stature. *Journal of Higher Education Management, 6,* 7–28.

Alfred, R. L., and Weissman, J. (1988). *Public image and the university.* ERIC Digest. [http://www.ericdigests.org/pre-9210/public.htm].

Allaire, Y., and Firsirotu, M. E. (1984). Theories of organizational culture. *Organizational Studies, 5,* 193–226.

Alles, M., and Datar, S. (2002, June). Control implications of worker identification with firm sales success. *Management Accounting Research, 13,* 173–190.

Altman, Y., and Baruch, Y. (1998). Cultural theory and organizations: Analytical method and cases. *Organization Studies, 19,* 769–785.

Alvesson, M., and Berg, P.-O. (1992). *Corporate culture and organizational symbolism.* Berlin: DeGruyter.

Ambler, T. (1999, August 12). The day has come to put brand equities on our balance sheets. *Marketing, 14,* 12–14.

Arens, W. (1976). Professional football: An American symbol and ritual. In W. Arens and S. P. Montague (Eds.), *The American dimension: Cultural myths and realities* (pp. 3–14). Port Washington, NY: Alfred Publishing.

Arnold, D. (1992). *Handbook of brand management.* London: The Economist Books.

Arnott, D. (2000). *Corporate cults: The insidious lure of the all-consuming organization.* New York: American Management Association.

Ashby, F. C. (1999). *Revitalize your corporate culture: Powerful ways to transform your company into a high-performance organization.* Houston: Cashman Dudley.

Ashforth, B. E., and Mael, F. (1989). Social identity theory and the organization. *Academy of Management Review, 14,* 20–39.

Ashkanasy, N. M., Broadfoot, L. E., and Flakus, S. (2000). Questionnaire measures of cultures. In N. M. Ashkanasy, C. P. Wilderom, and M. F. Peterson (Eds.), *Handbook of organizational culture and climate* (pp. 131–146). Thousand Oaks, CA: Sage.

Ashkanasy, N. M., Wilderom, C. P., and Peterson, M. F. (2000). Introduction. In N. M. Ashkanasy, C. P. Wilderom, and M. F. Peterson (Eds.), *Handbook of organizational culture and climate* (pp. 1–18). Thousand Oaks, CA: Sage.

Astin, A. W. (1993, January). An empirical typology of college students. *Journal of College Student Development, 34,* 36–46.

Austin, A. E. (1990). Faculty cultures, faculty values. In E. G. Tierney (Ed.), *Assessing academic climates and cultures* (pp. 61–74). San Francisco: Jossey-Bass.

Baird, L. L. (1988). The college environment revisited: A review of research and theory. In J. C. Smart (Ed.), *Higher education: Handbook of theory and research* (Vol. 4, pp. 1–52). New York: Agathon Press.

Baird, L. L. (1993). Learning from research on student outcomes. In S. Kormives, D. B. Woodward, and Associates, *Student services: A handbook for the profession* (3rd ed.). San Francisco: Jossey-Bass.

Baldwin, R. G., and Thelin, J. R. (1990). Thanks for the memories: The fusion of quantitative and qualitative research on college students and the college experience. In J. C. Smart (Ed.), *Higher education: Handbook of theory and research* (Vol. 6, pp. 337–360). New York: Agathon Press.

Bartel, C. A. (2001, September). Social comparisons in boundary-spanning work: Effects of community outreach on members' organizational identity and identification. *Administrative Science Quarterly, 46,* 379–413.

Bate, P., Khan, R., and Pye, A. (2000, March/April). Towards a culturally sensitive approach to organization structuring: Where organization design meets organization development. *Organization Science, 11,* 197–211.

Baumard, P., and Starbuck, W. H. (2001). Where are organizational cultures going? In C. L. Cooper, S. Cartwright, and P. C. Earley (Eds.), *The international handbook of organizational culture and climate* (pp. 521–532). New York: Wiley.

Becher, T. and Trowler, P. R. (2001). *Academic tribes and territories: Intellectual enquiry and the culture of disciplines.* Buckingham, UK: Society for Research into Higher Education and Open University Press.

Bergami, M., and Bagozzi, R. P. (2000, December). Self-categorization, affective commitment and group self-esteem as distinct aspects of social identity in the organization. *British Journal of Social Psychology, 39,* 555–577.

Bergquist, W. (1992). *The four cultures of the academy.* San Francisco: Jossey-Bass.

Beyer, J. H., Hannah, D. R., and Milton, L. P. (2000). Ties that bind: Culture and organizational attachment. In N. M. Ashkanasy, C. P. Wilderom, and M. F. Peterson (Eds.), *Handbook of organizational culture and climate* (pp. 323–339). Thousand Oaks, CA: Sage.

Bhattacharya, C. B., and Elsbach, K. D. (2002, Spring). Us versus them: The roles of organizational identification and disidentification in social marketing initiatives. *Journal of Public Policy and Marketing, 21,* 26–36.

Biglan, A. (1973). Relationships between subject matter characteristics and the structure and output of university departments. *Journal of Applied Psychology, 57*(3), 204–213.

Birnbaum, R. (1988). *How colleges work: The cybernetics of academic organization and leadership.* San Francisco: Jossey-Bass.

Blackston, M. (1995, July). The qualitative dimension of brand equity. *Journal of Advertising Research, 35,* 2–7.

Blau, P. M. (1973). *The organization of academic work.* New York: Wiley.

Bluedorn, A. C. (2000). Time and organizational culture. In N. M. Ashkanasy, C. P. Wilderom, and M. F. Peterson (Eds.), *Handbook of organizational culture and climate* (pp. 117–128). Thousand Oaks, CA: Sage.

Bok, D. (1986). *Higher learning.* Cambridge, MA: Harvard University Press.

Bolman, L., and Deal, T. (1997). *Reframing organizations: Artistry, choice, and leadership* (2nd ed.). San Francisco: Jossey-Bass.

Bolton, C. D., and Kammeyer, K.C.W. (1972). Campus cultures, role orientations, and social types. In K. Feldman (Ed.), *College and student: Selected readings in the social psychology of higher education* (pp. 377–391). New York: Pergamon Press.

Bowen, H. R. (1991). Goals: The intended outcomes of higher education. In J. Bess (Ed.), *Foundations of American higher education* (pp. 54–76). New York: Simon & Schuster Custom Publishing.

Bresler, W. (1989). The concern about community. *Educational Record, 70,* 5.

Brickson, S. (2000a, January). Exploring identity: Where are we now? *Academy of Management Review, 25,* 147–148.

Brickson, S. (2000b, January). The impact of identity orientation: Individual and organizational outcomes in demographically diverse settings. *Academy of Management Review, 25,* 82–101.

Butler, C. L., and Earley, P. C. (2001). Multinational groups and the structuration of organizational culture: A sociological perspective. In C. L. Cooper, S. Cartwright, and P. C. Earley (Eds.), *The international handbook of organizational culture and climate* (pp. 53–83). New York: Wiley.

Calhoun, D. (1987). *Sport, culture and personality.* Champaign, IL: Human Kinetics Publishers.

Cameron, K. S., and Ettington, D. R. (1988). The conceptual foundations of organizational culture. In J. C. Smart (Ed.), *Higher education: Handbook of theory and research* (Vol. 4, pp. 356–396). New York: Agathon Press.

Cameron, K. S., and Quinn, R. E. (1999). *Diagnosing and changing organizational culture.* Reading, MA: Addison-Wesley.

Campbell, M. C. (2002, May). Building brand equity. *International Journal of Medical Marketing, 2,* 208–218.

Chaffee, E. E., and Tierney, W. S. (1988). *Collegiate culture and leadership strategies.* New York: Macmillan.

Chan, A. (1997). Corporate culture of a clan organization. *Management Decision, 35,* 94–99.

Chaney, G. (1993). On the various and changing meanings of organized membership: A field study of organizational identification. *Communications Monographs, 50,* 342–362.

Chaudhuri, A. (2002, May/June). How brand reputation affects the advertising-brand equity link. *Journal of Advertising Research, 42,* 33–43.

Chickering, A. W., and Reisser, L. (1993). *Education and identity* (2nd ed.). San Francisco: Jossey-Bass.

Chreim, S. (2002, September). Influencing organizational identification during major change: A communication-based perspective. *Human Relations, 55,* 1117–1137.

Cialdini, R. B., and others. (1976). Basking in reflected glory: Three football field studies. *Journal of Personality and Social Psychology, 34,* 366–375.

Clark, B. R. (1970). *The distinctive college: Reed, Antioch, and Swarthmore.* Chicago: Aldine.

Clark, B. R. (1972). The organizational saga in higher education. *Administrative Science Quarterly, 17,* 178–184.

Clark, B. R. (1981). Belief and loyalty in college organization. *Journal of Higher Education, 42,* 499–520.

Clark, B. R. (1987). *The academic life: Small worlds, different worlds.* Princeton, NJ: Princeton University Press.

Clark, B. R., and Trow, M. (1966). The organizational context. In T. M. Newcomb and E. K. Wilson (Eds.), *College peer groups and prospects for research* (pp. 17–70). Chicago: Aldine.

Cobb-Walgren, C. J., Ruble, C. A., and Donthu, N. (1995). Brand equity, brand performance, and purchase intent. *Journal of Advertising, 24, Journal of Advertising, 24*(3), 25–40.

Cohen, M. D., and March, J. G. (1974). *Leadership and ambiguity.* New York: McGraw-Hill.

Collins, J. (2001). *Good to great: Why some companies make the leap . . . and others don't.* New York: Harper Business.

Collins, J. C., and Porras, J. I. (1996). *Built to last: Successful habits of visionary companies.* New York: Harper Business.

Cooke, R. A., and Szumal, J. L. (2000). Using the organizational culture inventory to understand the operating culture of organizations. In N. M. Ashkanasy, C. P. Wilderom, and M. F. Peterson (Eds.), *Handbook of organizational culture and climate* (pp. 147–163). Thousand Oaks, CA: Sage.

Cooper, C. S., Cartwright, S., and Earley, P. C. (Eds.). (2001). *The international handbook of organizational culture and climate.* New York: Wiley.

Cravens, K., Oliver, E. G., and Ramamoorti, S. (2003). The reputation index: Measuring and managing corporate reputation. *European Management Journal, 21,* 200–212.

Dandridge, T. C. (1983). Symbols' function and use. In L. R. Pondy, P. J. Frost, G. Morgan, and T. C. Dandridge (Eds.), *Organizational symbolism.* Greenwich, CT: JAI.

Dandridge, T. C. (1985). The life stages of a symbol: When symbols work and when they can't. In P. J. Frost, L. P. Moore, M. R. Louis, C. C. Lundberg, and J. Martin (Eds.), *Organizational culture* (pp. 141–154). Beverly Hills, CA: Sage.

Dandridge, T. C., Mitroff, I., and Joyce, W. F. (1980). Organizational symbolism: A topic to expand organizational analysis. *Academy of Management Review, 5,* 77–82.

Davey, K. M., and Symon, G. (2001). Recent approaches to the qualitative analysis of organizational culture. In C. L. Cooper, S. Cartwright, and P. Earley (Eds.), *The international handbook of organizational culture and climate* (pp. 123–142). New York: Wiley.

Deal, T. E., and Kennedy, A. A. (1982). *Corporate cultures: The rites and rituals of corporate life.* Reading, MA: Addison-Wesley.

Deal, T. E., and Kennedy, A. A. (1983). Culture: A new look through old lenses. *Journal of Applied Behavioral Sciences, 19,* 497–505.

Denison, D. (2001). Organizational culture: Can it be a key lever for driving organizational change? In C. L. Cooper, S. Cartwright, and P. Earley (Eds.), *The international handbook of organizational culture and climate* (pp. 347–374). New York: Wiley.

Deshpande, R., and Parasuaraman, A. (1986, May/June). Linking corporate culture to strategic planning. *Business Horizons, 29,* 28–37.

Detert, J. R., Schroeder, R. G., and Mauriel, J. J. (2000). A framework for linking culture and improvement initiatives in organizations. *Academy of Management Review, 25,* 850–863.

Dey, E. L., and Hurtado, S. (1994). College students in changing contexts. In P. G. Altbach, R. O. Berdahl, and P. J. Gumport (Eds.), *Higher education in American society* (3rd ed., pp. 249–268). Amherst, NY: Prometheus Books.

Diamond, M. (1993). *The unconscious life of organizations: Interpreting organization identity.* Westport, CT: Quorum Books.

Dillon, W. R., Madden, T. J., Kirmani, A., and Mukherjee, S. (2001). Understanding the role of brand-specific associations and general brand impressions in customer-based brand equity. *Journal of Marketing Research, 38,* 415–430.

Dubrow, G. (2003). *It's just the way things are done here: The role of institutional culture in the process of general education curriculum reform.* Doctoral dissertation, University of Pennsylvania (UMI No. 3087392).

Dukerich, J. M., and Carter, S. M. (2000). Distorted images and reputation repair. In M. Schultz, M. J. Hatch, and M. Holten Larsen (Eds.), *The expressive organization: Linking identity, reputation, and the corporate brand* (pp. 97–114). New York: Oxford University Press.

Dunbar, R., and Garud, R. (2001). Culture-in-the-making in telework settings. In C. L. Cooper, S. Cartwright, and P. Earley (Eds.), *The international handbook of organizational culture and climate* (pp. 573–587). New York: Wiley.

Duncan, W. J. (1989). Organizational culture: Getting a fix on an elusive concept. *Academy of Management Executive, 3,* 229–236.

Dutton, J. E., and Dukerich, J. M. (1991). Keeping an eye on the mirror: Image and identity in organizational adaptation. *Academy of Management Journal, 34,* 517–554.

Dutton, J. E., Dukerich, J. M., and Harquail, C. V. (1994). Organizational images and member identification. *Administrative Science Quarterly, 39,* 239–263.

Dyson, P., Farr, A., and Hollis, N. S. (1996). Understanding, measuring, and using brand equity. *Journal of Advertising Research, 36,* 9–21.

Eckel, P., Green, M., Hill, B., and Mallon, W. (1999). *Taking charge of change: A primer for colleges and universities.* Washington, DC: American Council on Education.

El-Khawas, E. (1996). Student diversity on today's campuses. In S. R. Komives, D. B. Woodard, Jr., and Associates (Eds.), *Student services: A handbook for the profession* (3rd ed., pp. 64–80). San Francisco: Jossey-Bass.

Elsbach, K. D., and Sutton, R. I. (1992). Acquiring organization legitimacy through illegitimate actions: A marriage of institutional and impression management. *Academy of Management Journal, 35,* 699–738.

Evans, N. J. (1996). Theories of student development. In S. R. Komives, D. B. Woodard, Jr., and Associates (Eds.), *Student services: A handbook for the profession* (3rd ed., pp. 164–187). San Francisco: Jossey-Bass.

Faircloth, J. B., Capella, L. M., and Alford, B. L. (2001, Summer). The effect of brand attitude and brand image on brand equity. *Journal of Marketing Theory and Practice, 9,* 61–75.

Fairfield-Sonn, J. W. (2001). *Corporate culture and the quality organization.* Westport, CT: Quorum Books.

Feldman, S. P. (1999, June). The leveling of organizational culture: Egalitarianism in critical postmodern organization theory. *Journal of Applied Behavioral Science, 35,* 228–244.

Fineman, S. (1993). Organizations as emotional arenas. In S. Fineman (Ed.), *Emotion in organizations* (pp. 9–35). Thousand Oaks, CA: Sage.

Fiol, C. M. (2002, November/December). Capitalizing on paradox: The role of language in transforming organizational identities. *Organization Science, 13,* 653–666.

Flynn, F. J., and Chatman, J. A. (2001). Strong cultures and innovation: Oxymoron or opportunity? In C. L. Cooper, S. P. Cartwright, and C. Earley (Eds.), *The international handbook of organizational culture and climate* (pp. 263–288). New York: Wiley.

Fombrun, C. J. (1996). *Reputation: Realizing value from the corporate image.* Cambridge, MA: Harvard Business School Press.

Fombrun, C. J., and Rindova, V. R. (2000). The road to transparency: Reputation management at Royal Dutch Shell. In M. Schultz, M. J. Hatch, and M. Holten Larsen (Eds.), *The expressive organization: Linking identity, reputation, and the corporate brand* (pp. 77–96). New York: Oxford University Press.

Foreman, P., and Whetten, D. A. (2002, November/December). Members' identification with multiple-identity organizations. *Organization Science, 13,* 618–635.

Frank, K. A., and Fahrbach, K. (1999, May/June). Organization culture as a complex system: Balance and information in models of influence and selection. *Organization Science, 10,* 253–277.

Franzen, G. (1999). *Brands and advertising: How advertising effectiveness influences brand equity.* Henley-on-Thames, UK: Admap.

Frost, P. J. (Ed.). (1985). *Organizational culture.* Beverly Hills, CA: Sage.

Frost, P. J., Moore, L. F., Louis, M. R., and Lundberg, C. C. (1985). An allegorical view of organizational culture. In P. J. Frost and others (Eds.), *Organizational culture* (pp. 13–23). Beverly Hills, CA: Sage.

Gabriel, Y. (2000). *Storytelling in organizations: Facts, fictions, and fantasies.* New York: Oxford University Press.

Gaff, J. G., and Wilson, R. C. (1971). Faculty cultures and interdisciplinary studies. *Journal of Higher Education, 42,* 186–201.

Gagliardi, P. (1990). Artifacts as pathways and remains of organizational life. In P. Gagliardi (Ed.), *Symbols and artifacts: Views of the corporate landscape* (pp. 3–40). New York: deGruyter.

Gagliardi, P. (1996). Exploring the aesthetic side of organizational life. In S. R. Clegg, C. Hardy, and W. R. Nord (Eds.), *The handbook of organizational studies* (pp. 565–580). Thousand Oaks, CA: Sage.

Gallagher, R. S. (2003). *The soul of an organization: Understanding the values that drive successful corporate cultures.* Chicago: Dearborn Trade Publications.

Garbett, T. (1988). *How to build a corporation's identity and protect its image.* Lexington, MA: D. C. Heath.

Gardner, J. W. (1989, Fall). Building community. *Kettering Review,* 73–81.

Geertz, C. (1972). Deep play: Notes on the Balinese cockfight. *Daedalus, 101,* 1–37.

Geertz, C. (1973). *The interpretation of cultures.* New York: Basic Books.

Gherrardi, S. (1995). *Gender, symbolism and organizational cultures.* Thousand Oaks, CA: Sage.

Gilley, J. W., and Hawkes, R. T., Jr. (1990). Nontraditional students: A changing student body redefines community. *Educational Record, 70,* 33–35.

Ginzel, L. E., Kramer, R. M., and Sutton, R. I. (1993). Organizational impression management as a reciprocal influence process: The neglected role of the organizational audience. In L. L. Cummings and B. Staw (Eds.), *Research in organizational behavior* (Vol. 15, pp. 227–266). Greenwich, CT: JAI Press.

Gioia, D. A., and Thomas, J. B. (1996, September). Identity, image, and issue interpretation: Sensemaking during strategic change in academia. *Administrative Science Quarterly, 41,* 370–403.

Gluckman, M., and Gluckman, M. (1983). On drama, and games, and athletic contests. In J. C. Harris and R. J. Parks (Eds.), *Play games and sports in cultural context.* Champaign, IL: Human Kinetics.

Glynn, M. A., and Abzug, R. (2002, February). Institutionalizing identity: Symbolic isomorphism and organizational names. *Academy of Management, 45,* 267–280.

Goffee, R., and Jones, G. (2001). Culture from a sociological perspective. In C. L. Cooper, S. P. Cartwright, and C. Earley (Eds.), *The international handbook of organizational culture and climate* (pp. 3–20). New York: Wiley.

Gouldner, A. G. (1957). Cosmopolitans and locals: Toward an analysis of latent social roles. *Administrative Science Quarterly, 2,* 281–306.

Grace, J. D., and Leslie, L. L. (1990). Research on institutional advancement: Emerging patterns and perspectives. *Review of Higher Education, 13,* 425–432.

Hall, D. T., Schneider, B., and Nygren, H. T. (1970). Personal factors in organizational identification. *Administrative Science Quarterly, 17,* 340–350.

Hall, S. (1990). Cultural identity and diaspora. In J. Rutherford (Ed.), *Identity: Community, culture, difference* (pp. 222–237). London: Lawrence & Wishart.

Hall, S. (1996). Introduction: Who needs identity? In S. Hall and P. du Gay (Eds.), *Questions of cultural identity* (pp. 1–18). Thousand Oaks, CA: Sage.

Hall, S. (1997). The work of representation. In S. Hall (Ed.), *Representation: Cultural representations and signifying practices* (pp. 13–75). Thousand Oaks, CA: Sage.

Harris, J. (1983). Sport and ritual: A macroscopic comparison of form. In J. C. Harris and R. J. Parks (Eds.), *Play games and sports in cultural context* (pp. 177–189). Champaign, IL: Human Kinetics.

Harris, L. C., and Ogbonna, E. (2002, March). The unintended consequences of culture interventions: A study of unexpected outcomes. *British Journal of Management, 13,* 31–49.

Hartley, M. (2002). *A call to purpose: Mission-centered change at three liberal arts colleges.* New York: RoutledgeFalmer.

Hatch, M. J. (2000). The cultural dynamics of organizing and change. In N. M. Ashkanasy, C. P. Wilderom, and M. F. Peterson (Eds.), *Handbook of organizational culture and climate* (pp. 245–260). Thousand Oaks, CA: Sage.

Hatch, M. J., and Schultz, M. (2000). Scaling the tower of Babel: Relational differences between identity, image, and culture in organizations. In M. Schultz, M. J. Hatch, and M. Holten Larsen (Eds.), *The expressive organization: Linking identity, reputation, and the corporate brand* (pp. 11–35). New York: Oxford University Press.

Hearn, J., and Heydinger, R. (1985). Scanning the university's external environment. *Journal of Higher Education, 46*(4), 429–445.

Hedberg, B., and Maravelias, C. (2001). Organizational culture and imaginary organizations. In C. L. Cooper, S. Cartwright, and P. Earley (Eds.), *The international handbook of organizational culture and climate* (pp. 587–600). New York: Wiley.

Helms Mills, J. C., and Mills, A. J. (2000). Rules, sensemaking, formative contexts, and discourse in the gendering of organizational change. In N. M. Ashkanasy, C. P. Wilderom, and M. F. Peterson (Eds.), *Handbook of organizational culture and climate* (pp. 55–71). Thousand Oaks, CA: Sage.

Heracleous, L. (2001, December). An ethnographic study of culture in the context of organizational change. *Journal of Applied Behavioral Science, 37,* 426–446.

Hermalin, B. E. (2001). Economics and corporate culture. In C. L. Cooper, S. P. Cartwright, and C. Earley (Eds.), *The international handbook of organizational culture and climate* (pp. 217–262). New York: Wiley.

Hoeffler, S., and Keller, K. L. (2002, Spring). Building brand equity through corporate societal marketing. *Journal of Public Policy and Marketing, 21,* 78–89.

Hofstede, G. (1998, January). Identifying organizational subcultures: An empirical approach. *Journal of Management Studies, 35,* 1–12.

Hogg, M. A., and Terry, D. J. (2000, January). The dynamic, diverse, and variable faces of organizational identity. *Academy of Management Review, 25,* 150–152.

Horowitz, H. L. (1987). *Campus life: Undergraduate cultures from the end of the eighteenth century to the present.* Chicago: University of Chicago Press.

Hummon, D. M. (1994). College slang revisited: Language, culture and undergraduate life. *Journal of Higher Education, 65,* 75–98.

Humphreys, M., and Brown, A. D. (2002). Narratives of organizational identity and identification: A case study of hegemony and resistance. *Organizational Studies, 23,* 421–447.

Itzin, C., and Newman, J. (Eds.). (1995). *Gender, culture, and organizational change: Putting theory into practice.* New York: Routledge.

Jassawalla, A. R., and Sashittal, H. C. (2002, August). Cultures that support product-innovation processes. *Academy of Management Executive, 16,* 42–54.

Jones, M. O. (1996). *Studying organizational symbolism: What, how, why?* Thousand Oaks, CA: Sage.

Kafka, J. S. (1983). Challenge and confirmation in ritual action. *Psychiatry, 46,* 31–50.

Kahn, W. A. (1989). Toward a sense of organizational humor: Implications for organizational diagnosis and change. *Journal of Applied Behavioral Sciences, 25,* 45–63.

Kamens, D. H. (1977). Legitimating myths and educational organizations: The relationship between organizational ideology and formal structure. *American Sociological Review, 42,* 208–219.

Kanter, R. M. (1972). *Commitment and community.* Cambridge, MA: Harvard University Press.

Kapferer, J.-N. (1992). *Strategic brand management: New approaches to creating and evaluating brand equity.* New York: Free Press.

Kapferer, J.-N. (2000). *Strategic brand management: New approaches to creating and evaluating brand equity.* Collingdale, PA: DIANE Publishing.

Kapferer, J.-N. (2001). *[Re]inventing the brand: Can top brands survive the new market realities?* London: Kogan Page.

Katz, D., and Kahn, R. L. (1966). *The social psychology of organizations.* New York: Wiley.

Keller, K. L. (2003). *Strategic brand management: Building, measuring, and managing brand equity* (2nd ed.). Upper Saddle River, NJ: Prentice Hall.

Kellogg Commission on the Future of State and Land-Grant Universities. (2000, January). Returning to our roots: Toward a coherent campus culture. Washington, DC: National Association of State Universities and Land-Grant Colleges.

Kerr, C. (2001). *The uses of the university.* Cambridge, MA: Harvard University Press.

Kezar, A. J. (2001). *Understanding and facilitating change in higher education in the 21st century.* San Francisco: Jossey-Bass.

Kezar, A. J., and Eckel, P. (2002). *Taking the reins: Institutional transformation in higher education.* Phoenix: ACE/Oryx Press.

Kilduff, M., and Corley, K. G. (2000). Social network theory and measuring performance. In N. M. Ashkanasy, C. P. Wilderom, and M. F. Peterson (Eds.), *Handbook of organizational culture and climate* (pp. 211–222). Thousand Oaks, CA: Sage.

Kuh, G. D. (1991). Snapshots of campus community. *Educational Record, 72,* 40–44.

Kuh, G. D. (1993a). Assessing campus environments. In M. Barr (Ed.), *Handbook of student affairs administration* (pp. 30–48). San Francisco: Jossey-Bass.

Kuh, G. D. (1993b, Fall). Ethos: Its influence on student learning. *Liberal Education,* 22–31.

Kuh, G. D., and Hall, J. E. (1993). Cultural perspectives in student affairs. In G. D. Kuh (Ed.), *Cultural perspectives in students affairs* (pp. 1–20). Lanham, MD: University Press of America.

Kuh, G. D., Schuh, J., and Whitt, E. (1991). *Involving colleges: Successful approaches to fostering student learning and development outside the classroom.* San Francisco: Jossey-Bass.

Kuh, G. D., and Whitt, E. J. (1988). *The invisible tapestry: Culture in American colleges and universities.* ASHE-ERIC Higher Education Reports. Washington, DC: Association for the Study of Higher Education.

Kuhn, T., and Nelson, N. (2002, August). Reengineering identity: A case study of multiplicity and duality in organizational identification. *Management Communication Quarterly, 16,* 5–38.

Labianca, G., Fairbank, J. F., Thomas, J. B., and Gioia, D. A. (2001, May/June). Emulation in academia: Balancing structure and identity. *Organization Science, 12,* 312–330.

Lakomski, G. (2001). Organizational change, leadership and learning: Culture as cognitive process. *International Journal of Educational Management, 15,* 135–151.

Larsen, M. H. (2000). Managing the corporate story. In M. Schultz, M. J. Hatch, and M. Holten Larsen (Eds.), *The expressive organization: Linking identity, reputation, and the corporate brand* (pp. 196–207). New York: Oxford University Press.

Levinson, H. (1965). Reciprocation: The relationship between man and organization. *Administrative Science Quarterly, 9,* 370–390.

Lewis, D. (2002). Five years on: The organizational culture saga revisited. *Leadership and Organization Development Journal, 23,* 280–287.

Louis, M. R. (1983). Organizations as culture-bearing milieux. In L. R. Pondy, P. J. Frost, G. Morgan, and T. C. Dandridge (Eds.), *Organizational symbolism* (pp. 39–54). Greenwich, CT: JAI.

Lund, D. B. (2003). Organizational culture and job satisfaction. *Journal of Business and Industrial Marketing, 18,* 216–236.

Lundberg, C. C. (1990). Surfacing organizational culture. *Journal of Management Psychology, 5,* 19–26.

Lundberg, C. C. (2001). Working with cultures: Social rules perspective. In C. L. Cooper, S. Cartwright, and P. C. Earley (Eds.), *The international handbook of organizational culture and climate* (pp. 53–83). New York: Wiley.

Mackay, M. M. (2001). Evaluation of brand equity measures: Further empirical results. *Journal of Product and Brand Management, 10,* 38–51.

Mael, F., and Ashforth, B. E. (1992). Alumni and their alma mater: A partial test of the reformulated model of organizational identification. *Journal of Organizational Behavior, 13,* 103–123.

Major, D. A. (2000). Effective newcomer socialization into high-performance organizational cultures. In N. M. Ashkanasy, C. P. Wilderom, and M. F. Peterson (Eds.), *Handbook of organizational culture and climate* (pp. 355–369). Thousand Oaks, CA: Sage.

Manning, K. (1993). Properties of institutional culture. In G. D. Kuh (Ed.), *Cultural perspective in student affairs work* (pp. 21–36). Lanham, MD: University Press of America.

March, J. G., and Simon, H. A. (1963). *Organizations* (2nd ed.). New York: Wiley.

Markus, K. A. (2000). Twelve testable assertions about cultural dynamics and the reproduction of organizational culture. In N. M. Ashkanasy, C. P. Wilderom, and M. F. Peterson (Eds.). *Handbook of organizational culture and climate* (pp. 297–308). Thousand Oaks, CA: Sage.

Martin, J. (1992). *Cultures in organizations: Three perspectives.* New York: Oxford University Press.

Martin, J. (2002). *Organizational culture: Mapping the terrain.* Thousand Oaks, CA: Sage.

Martin, J., Feldman, M. S., Hatch, M. J., and Sitkin, S. B. (1983). The uniqueness paradox in organizational stories. *Administrative Science Quarterly, 28,* 438–452.

Martin, J., and Frost, P. (1990). The organizational culture war games: A struggle for intellectual dominance. In S. R. Clegg, C. Hardy, and W. R. Nord (Eds.), *The handbook of organizational studies* (pp. 599–621). Thousand Oaks, CA: Sage.

Martin, J., and Powers, M. E. (1983). Truth or corporate propaganda: The value of a good war story. In L. R. Pondy, P. J. Frost, G. Morgan, and T. C. Dandridge (Eds.), *Organizational symbolism* (pp. 93–107). Greenwich, CT: JAI.

Martin, J., and Siehl, C. (1983). Organizational culture and counterculture: An uneasy symbiosis. *Organizational Dynamics, 12,* 52–64.

Martin, R., and Epitropaki, O. (2001, July). Role of organizational identification on implicit leadership theories. *Transformational Leadership and Work Attitudes, 4,* 247–262.

Masland, A. T. (1982). Simulators, myth, and ritual in higher education. Paper presented at a meeting of the Association for Institutional Research, Denver, CO. (ED 220 048)

Masland, A. T. (1985). Organizational culture in the study of higher education. *Review of Higher Education, 8,* 157–168.

Mason, D. (2003). Tailoring scenario planning to the company culture. *Strategy and Leadership, 31,* 25–28.

McKnight, D. H., and Webster, J. (2001). Collaborative insight or privacy invasion? Trust climate as a lens for understanding acceptance of awareness systems. In C. L. Cooper,

S. Cartwright, and P. Earley (Eds.), *The international handbook of organizational culture and climate* (pp. 533–556). New York: Wiley.

Melchiori, G. S. (1990). Managing institutional image. *Journal of Higher Education Management, 6,* 45–58.

Merton, R. K. (1968). *Social theory and social structure.* New York: Free Press.

Michael, S. O. (1997). American higher education system: Consumerism versus professionalism. *International Journal of Educational Management, 11,* 117–130.

Michela, J. L., and Burke, W. W. (2000). Organizational culture and climate in transformations for quality and innovation. In N. M. Ashkanasy, C. P. Wilderom, and M. F. Peterson (Eds.), *Handbook of organizational culture and climate* (pp. 225–244). Thousand Oaks, CA: Sage.

Moffitt, M. (1991). *Coming of age in New Jersey: College and American culture.* New Brunswick, NJ: Rutgers University Press.

Montague, S. P., and Morris, R. (1976). Football games and rock concerts: The ritual enactment of American success models. In W. Arens and S. P. Montague (Eds.), *The American dimension: Cultural myths and realities* (pp. 33–52). Port Washington, NY: Alfred Publishing.

Moore, S. F., and Myerhoff, B. (1977). Introduction. Secular ritual: Forms and meaning. In S. Moore and B. Myerhoff (Eds.), *Secular ritual.* Netherlands: Van Gorcum.

Morgan, G. (1996). *Images of organizations.* Thousand Oaks, CA: Sage.

Morgan, G., Frost, P. J., and Pondy, L. R. (1983). Organizational symbolism. In L. R. Pondy, P. J. Frost, G. Morgan, and T. C. Dandridge (Eds.), *Organizational symbolism* (pp. 55–65). Greenwich, CT: JAI.

Myers, C. A. (2003). Managing brand equity: A look at the impact of attributes. *Journal of Product and Brand Management, 12,* 39–49.

Nadler, D. A., Thies, P. K., and Nadler, M. B. (2001). Cultural change in the strategic enterprise: Lessons from the field. In C. L. Cooper, S. Cartwright, and P. Earley (Eds.), *The international handbook of organizational culture and climate* (pp. 309–324). New York: Wiley.

Neumann, A. (1995). Context, cognition, and culture: A case study of collegiate leadership and cultural change. *American Educational Research Journal, 32,* 251–279.

Nilson, T. (2003). *Customize the brand: Make it more desirable—and profitable.* New York: Wiley.

Ogbonna, E., and Harris, L. C. (1998). Organizational culture: It's not what you think. *Journal of General Management, 23,* 35–48.

Ogbor, J. O. (2001). Critical theory and the hegemony of corporate culture. *Journal of Organizational Change Management, 14,* 590–608.

O'Reilly, C., and Chatman, J. (1986). Organizational commitment and psychological attainment: The effects of compliance identification and prosocial behavior. *Journal of Applied Psychology, 71,* 492–499.

Ouchi, W. G. (1982). *Theory Z: How American business can meet the Japanese challenge.* New York: Avon.

Ouchi, W. G., and Wilkins, A. L. (1985). Organizational culture. *Annual Review of Sociology, 11,* 457–483.

Pace, C. R. (1962). Methods of describing college cultures. *Teachers College Record, 63,* 267–277.

Parker, M. (2000). *Organizational culture and identity: Unity and division at work.* Thousand Oaks, CA: Sage.

Parameswaran, R., and Glowacka, A. E. (1995). University image: An information processing perspective. *Journal of Marketing for Higher Education, 6*(2), 41–56.

Payne, R. L. (2001). A three-dimensional framework for analyzing and assessing culture/climate and its relevance to cultural change. In C. L. Cooper, S. P. Cartwright, and C. Earley (Eds.), *The international handbook of organizational culture and climate* (pp. 107–122). New York: Wiley.

Perrow, C. (1961). Organizational prestige: Some functions and dysfunctions. *American Journal of Sociology, 61,* 371–391.

Perrow, C. B. (1970). *Organizational analysis: A sociological view.* Belmont, CA: Brooks-Cole Publishing Company.

Peters, T., and Waterman, R. H., Jr. (1982). *In search of excellence.* New York: Harper.

Peterson, M. F., and Smith, P. B. (2000). Sources of meaning, organizations, and culture: Making sense of organizational events. In N. M. Ashkanasy, C. P. Wilderom, and M. F. Peterson (Eds.), *Handbook of organizational culture and climate* (pp. 101–116). Thousand Oaks, CA: Sage.

Peterson, M. W., and Spencer, M. G. (1990). Understanding academic culture and climate. *New Directions for Institutional Research, 68,* 3–18.

Peterson, M. W., and Spencer, M. G. (1993). Qualitative and quantitative approaches to academic culture: Do they tell us the same thing? In J. Smart (Ed.), *Higher education: Handbook of research and practice* (pp. 344–388). New York: Agathon Press.

Petromilli, M., Morrison, D., and Million, M. (2002). Brand architecture: Building brand portfolio value. *Strategy and Leadership, 8,* 22–28.

Pettigrew, A. M. (1979). On studying organizational cultures. *Administrative Science Quarterly, 24,* 570–581.

Pettigrew, A. M. (2000). Foreword. In N. M. Ashkanasy, C. P. Wilderom, and M. F. Peterson (Eds.), *Handbook of organizational culture and climate* (pp. xiii–xvi). Thousand Oaks, CA: Sage.

Pondy, L. R. (1983). The role of metaphors and myths in organizations and in the facilitation of change. In L. R. Pondy, P. J. Frost, G. Morgan, and T. C. Dandridge (Eds.), *Organizational symbolism* (pp. 157–166). Greenwich, CT: JAI.

Preston, P. W. (1997). *Political/cultural identity: Nations and citizens in a global era.* Thousand Oaks, CA: Sage.

Putnam, L. L., and Mumby, D. K. (1993). Organizations, emotion and the myth of rationality. In S. Fineman (Ed.), *Emotion in organizations* (pp. 36–57). Thousand Oaks, CA: Sage.

Putnam, L. L., Phillips, N., and Chapman, P. (1996). Metaphors of communication in organization. In S. R. Clegg, C. Hardy, and W. R. Nord (Eds.), *The handbook of organizational studies* (pp. 375–408). Thousand Oaks, CA: Sage.

Rafaeli, A., and Worline, M. (2000). Symbols in organizational culture. In N. M. Ashkanasy, C. P. Wilderom, and M. F. Peterson (Eds.), *Handbook of organizational culture and climate* (pp. 71–84). Thousand Oaks, CA: Sage.

Randall, T., Ulrich, K., and Reibstein, D. (1998). Brand equity and vertical product line extent. *Marketing Science, 17,* 356–379.

Ravasi, D., and van Rekom, J. (2003). Key issues in organizational identity and identification theory. *Corporate Reputation Review, 6,* 118–132.

Reuben, J. A. (1996). *The making of the modern university: Intellectual transformation and the marginalization of morality.* Chicago: University of Chicago Press.

Rhoads, R. A. (1995). Whales tales, dog piles, and beer goggles: An ethnographic case study of fraternity life. *Anthropology and Education Quarterly, 26,* 306–323.

Riesman, D. (1980). *On higher education: The academic enterprise in an era of rising student consumerism.* San Francisco: Jossey-Bass.

Rosenfeld, P., Giacalone, R. A., and Riordan, C. A. (1995). *Impression management in organizations: Theory, measurement, practice.* New York: Routledge.

Rousseau, D. M. (1998, May). Why workers still identify with organizations. *Journal of Organizational Behavior, 19,* 217–233.

Ruscio, K. (1987). Many sectors, many professions. In B. Clark (Ed.), *The academic profession: National, disciplinary and institutional settings.* Berkeley: University of California Press.

Rutherford, J. (1990). A place called home: Identity and the cultural politics of difference. In J. Rutherford (Ed.), *Identity: Community, culture, and difference* (pp. 9–27). London: Lawrence & Wishart.

Rydell, E. E. (1989). External relations. In A. R. Westley (Ed.), *Handbook of institutional advancement* (pp. 47–59). San Francisco: Jossey-Bass.

Sackmann, S. A. (1991). *Cultural knowledge in organizations: Exploring the collective mind.* Newbury Park, CA: Sage.

Sackmann, S. A. (1992). Culture and subcultures: An analysis of organizational knowledge. *Administrative Science Quarterly, 23,* 224–253.

Sackmann, S. A. (Ed.). (1997). *Cultural complexity in organizations: Inherent contrasts and contradictions.* Thousand Oaks, CA: Sage.

Sackmann, S. A. (2001). Cultural complexity in organizations: The value and limitations of qualitative methodology and approaches. In C. L. Cooper, S. P. Cartwright, and C. Earley (Eds.), *The international handbook of organizational culture and climate* (pp. 143–165). New York: Wiley.

Sanderson, A. R. (2001). Wealth of notions. *University of Chicago Magazine, 94.* [http://magazine.uchicago.edu/0122/features/].

Sathe, V., and Davidson, E. J. (2000). Toward a new conceptualization of cultural change. In N. M. Ashkanasy, C. P. Wilderom, and M. F. Peterson (Eds.), *Handbook of organizational culture and climate* (pp. 279–296). Thousand Oaks, CA: Sage.

Schein, E. (1992). *Organizational culture and leadership* (2nd ed.). San Francisco: Jossey-Bass.

Schein, E. (2000). Sense and nonsense about culture and climate. In N. M. Ashkanasy, C. P. Wilderom, and M. F. Peterson (Eds.), *Handbook of organizational culture and climate* (xxiii–xxx). Thousand Oaks, CA: Sage.

Schneider, B. (2000). The psychological life of organizations. In N. M. Ashkanasy, C. P. Wilderom, and M. F. Peterson (Eds.), *Handbook of organizational culture and climate* (pp. xvii–xxii). Thousand Oaks, CA: Sage.

Schneider, B., Bowen, D. E., Ehrhart, M. G., and Holcombe, K. M. (2000). The climate for service: Evolution of a construct. In N. M. Ashkanasy, C. P. Wilderom, and M. F. Peterson (Eds.), *Handbook of organizational culture and climate* (pp. 21–36). Thousand Oaks, CA: Sage.

Schultz, D. E. (2000, Spring). Understanding and measuring brand equity. *Marketing Management, 9,* 8–9.

Schultz, D. E. (2002, May/June). Mastering brand metrics. *Marketing Management, 11,* 8–9.

Scott, W. R. (2001). *Institutions and organizations* (2nd ed.). Thousand Oaks, CA: Sage.

Selame, E., and Selame, J. (1988). *Your company image: Building your identity and influence in the marketplace.* New York: Wiley.

Sevier, R. A. (1994). Image is everything: Strategies for measuring, changing, and maintaining your institution's image. *College and University, 69,* 60–75.

Sevier, R. A. (1998). *Integrated marketing for colleges, universities, and schools.* Washington, DC: Council for the Advancement and Support of Education.

Shaw, G. G. (2000). Planning and communicating using stories. In M. Schultz, M. J. Hatch, and M. Holten Larsen (Eds.), *The expressive organization: Linking identity, reputation, and the corporate brand* (pp. 182–195). New York: Oxford University Press.

Smart, J. C., and St. John, E. P. (1996, Fall). Organizational culture and effectiveness in higher education: A test of the "culture type" and "strong culture" hypotheses. *Educational Evaluation and Policy Analysis, 18,* 219–241.

Smith, F. L., and Keyton, J. (2001, November). Organizational storytelling. *Management Communication Quarterly, 15,* 149–182.

Sparrow, P. (2001). Developing diagnostics for high performance organizations. In C. L. Cooper, S. P. Cartwright, and C. Earley (Eds.), *The international handbook of organizational culture and climate* (pp. 85–106). New York: Wiley.

Spitzberg, I. J., and Thorndike, V. V. (1992). *Creating community on college campuses.* Albany: State University of New York Press.

Srinivasan, V. (2003). Organisational character: The key to transforming organisations of the future. *International Journal of Human Resources Development and Management, 3,* 29–38.

Stackman, R. W., Pinder, C. C., and Conner, P. E. (2000). Values lost: Redirecting research on values in the workplace. In N. M. Ashkanasy, C. P. Wilderom, and M. F. Peterson (Eds.), *Handbook of organizational culture and climate* (pp. 37–54). Thousand Oaks, CA: Sage.

Stein, M. (1983). Cult and sport: The case of Big Red. In J. C. Harris and R. J. Parks (Eds.), *Play games and sports in cultural context* (pp. 299–309). Champaign, IL: Human Kinetics.

The Uses of Institutional Culture

Stein, R. H. (1990). The issue of image. *Journal of Higher Education Management, 6*, 3–6.

Stern, S. (1988). A symbolic representation of organizational identity. In M. O. Jones, M. D. Moore, and R. C. Snyder (Eds.), *Inside organizations* (pp. 281–295). Newbury Park, CA: Sage.

Sun, H.-C. (2002). The relationship between organisational culture and its national culture: A case study. *International Journal of Human Resources Development and Management, 2*, 78–96.

Supphellen, M. (2000, Summer). Understanding core brand equity: Guidelines for in-depth elicitation of brand associations. *International Journal of Market Research, 42*, 319–338.

Sutton, C. D., and Harrison, A. W. (1993). Validity assessment of compliance, identification, and internalization as dimensions of organizational commitment. *Educational and Psychological Measurement, 53*, 217–224.

Terkla, D. G., and Pagano, M. F. (1993). Understanding institutional image. *Research in Higher Education, 34*, 11–22.

Thompson, K. R., and Luthans, F. (1990). Organizational culture: A behavioral perspective. In B. Schneider (Ed.), *Organizational culture and climate* (pp. 319– 344). San Francisco: Jossey-Bass.

Thornbury, J. (2003). Creating a living culture: The challenges for business leaders. *Corporate Governance, 3*, 68–79.

Tierney, W. G. (1988). Organizational culture in higher education: Defining the essentials. *Journal of Higher Education, 59*, 2–21.

Tierney, W. G. (1989). *Curricular landscapes, democratic vistas: Transformational leadership in higher education.* New York: Praeger.

Tierney, W. G. (1991). Ideology and identity in postsecondary institutions. In W. G. Tierney (Ed.), *Culture and ideology in higher education: Advancing a critical agenda* (pp. 35–58). New York: Praeger.

Tierney, W. G., and Rhoads, R. A. (1993). *Enhancing promotion, tenure, and beyond: Faculty socialization as a cultural process.* ASHE-ERIC Higher Education Report. Washington, DC: Association for the Study of Higher Education.

Toma, J. D. (1997, November/December). Alternative inquiry paradigms, faculty cultures, and the definition of academic lives. *Journal of Higher Education, 68*, 679–705.

Toma, J. D. (2003). *Football U.: Spectator sports in the life of the American university.* Ann Arbor: University of Michigan Press.

Toma, J. D., and Morphew, C. C. (2001, November). *The public liberal arts college: Case studies of institutions that have bucked the trend . . . and what it says about mission and market for all institutions.* Paper presented at the 2001 Association for the Study of Higher Education Annual Conference, Richmond, VA.

Trice, H. M. (1985). Rites and ceremonials in organizational cultures. *Research in the Sociology of Organizations, 4*, 221–270.

Trice, H. M., and Beyer, J. (1984). Studying organizational cultures through rites and ceremonials. *Academy of Management Review, 9*, 653–669.

Trice, H. M., and Beyer, J. (1993). *The cultures of work organizations*. Englewood Cliffs, NJ: Prentice Hall.

Trow, M. A. (1997). American higher education: Past, present, and future. In L. F. Goodchild and H. S. Wechsler (Eds.), *The history of higher education* (2nd ed., pp. 571–586). New York: Simon & Schuster Custom Publishing.

Tyrrell, M.W.D. (2000). Hunting and gathering in the early silicon age: Cyberspace, jobs, and the reformulation of organizational culture. In N. M. Ashkanasy, C. P. Wilderom, and M. F. Peterson (Eds.), *Handbook of organizational culture and climate* (pp. 85–100). Thousand Oaks, CA: Sage.

Van Auken, B. (2003). *Brand aid: An easy reference guide to solving your toughest branding problems and strengthening your market position*. New York: American Management Association.

Van Buskirk, W., and McGrath, D. (1999, June). Organizational cultures as holding environments: A psychodynamic look at organizational symbolism. *Human Relations, 52,* 805–832.

Van Gennep, A. (1960). *The rites of passage*. Chicago: University of Chicago Press.

Van Maanen, J., and Barley, S. R. (1985). Cultural organization: Fragments of a theory. In P. J. Frost, L. F. Moore, M. R. Louis, and C. C. Lundberg (Eds.), *Organizational culture* (pp. 31–54). Beverly Hills, CA: Sage.

Van Maanen, J., and Kunda, G. (1989). Real feelings: Emotional expression and organizational culture. In L. L. Cummings and B. M. Staw (Eds.), *Research in organizational behavior* (Vol. 11, pp. 43–103). Greenwich, CT: JAI.

van Riel, C.B.M. (2000). Corporate communication orchestrated by a sustainable corporate story. In M. Schultz, M. J. Hatch, and M. Holten Larsen (Eds.), *The expressive organization: Linking identity, reputation, and the corporate brand* (pp. 157–181). New York: Oxford University Press.

Virtanen, T. (2000). Commitment and the study of organizational climate and culture. In N. M. Ashkanasy, C. P. Wilderom, and M. F. Peterson (Eds.), *Handbook of organizational culture and climate* (339–354). Thousand Oaks, CA: Sage.

Wann, D. L., and Branscombe, N. R. (1990). Die-hard and fair-weather fans: Effects of identification on BIRGing and CORFing tendencies. *Journal of Sport and Social Issues, 14,* 103–117.

Washburn, J. H., and Plank, R. E. (2002, Winter). Measuring brand equity: An evaluation of a consumer-based brand equity scale. *Journal of Marketing Theory and Practice, 10,* 46–62.

Weber, M. (1947). *The theory of social and economic organization*. New York: Free Press.

Wee, T.T.T., and Ming, M.C.H. (2003, February). Leveraging on symbolic values and meanings in branding. *Journal of Brand Management, 10,* 208–218.

Weick, K. (1995). *Sensemaking in organizations*. Thousand Oaks, CA: Sage.

Whetten, D. A., and Mackey, A. (2002, December). A social actor conception of organizational identity and its implications for the study of organizational reputation. *Business and Society, 41,* 393–414.

Wiesenfeld, B., Raghuram, S., and Garud, R. (2001). Organizational identification among virtual workers: The role of need for affiliation and perceived work-based social support. *Journal of Management, 27*, 213–229.

Wilderom, C.P.M., Glunk, U., and Maslowski, R. (2000). Organizational culture as a predictor of organizational performance. In N. M. Ashkanasy, C. P. Wilderom, and M. F. Peterson (Eds.), *Handbook of organizational culture and climate* (pp. 193–210). Thousand Oaks, CA: Sage.

Wilensky, A. S., and Hansen, C. D. (2001, Fall). Understanding the work beliefs of nonprofit executives through organizational stories. *Human Resource Development Quarterly, 12*, 223–239.

Wiley, J. W., and Brooks, S. M. (2000). Measures of organizational culture. In N. M. Ashkanasy, C. P. Wilderom, and M. F. Peterson (Eds.), *Handbook of organizational culture and climate* (pp. 177–192). Thousand Oaks, CA: Sage.

Wilkins, A. L. (1983). Organizational stories as symbols which control the organization. In L. R. Pondy, P. J. Frost, G. Morgan, and T. C. Dandridge (Eds.), *Organizational symbolism* (pp. 81–92). Greenwich, CT: JAI.

Wilkins, A. L., and Ouchi, W. G. (1983). Efficient cultures: Exploring the relationship between culture and organizational performance. *Administrative Science Quarterly, 28*, 468–481.

Wood, L. (2000). Brands and brand equity: Definition and management. *Management Decision, 38*, 662–669.

Woodward, K. (Ed.). (1997). *Identity and difference.* Thousand Oaks, CA: Sage.

Wright, S. (1994). Culture in anthropology and organizational studies. In S. Wright (Ed.), *Anthropology of organizations.* New York: Routledge.

Yoo, B., Naveen, D., and Lee, S. (2000, Spring). An examination of selected marketing mix elements and brand equity. *Academy of Marketing Science Journal, 28*, 195–211.

Zammuto, R. F., Gifford, B., and Goodman, E. A. (2000). Organizations that stress control find change difficult. In N. M. Ashkanasy, C. P. Wilderom, and M. F. Peterson (Eds.), *Handbook of organizational culture and climate* (pp. 261–278). Thousand Oaks, CA: Sage.

Zemsky, R., Shaman, S., and Iannozzi, M. (1997, November/December). In search of strategic perspective: A tool for mapping the market in postsecondary education. *Change*, 23–38.

Name Index

A

Aaker, D. A., 4, 27, 30, 31
Abela, A., 31
Abzug, R., 7
Adler, P. A., 17
Adler, P., 17
Albert, S., 20, 24
Alford, B. L., 36
Alfred, R. L., 34
Allaire, Y., 43, 67
Alles, M., 24
Altman, Y., 42
Alvesson, M., 41, 42, 46
Ambler, T., 31
Arens, W., 71, 73
Arnott, D., 41
Ashby, F. C., 41, 46
Ashkanasy, N. M., 41, 44, 46
Ashforth, B. E., 21, 22
Astin, A. W., 54
Austin, A. E., 52

B

Bagozzi, R. P., 19
Baird, L. L., 58
Baldwin, R. G., 51
Barley, S. R., 42
Bartel, C. A., 24
Baruch, Y., 42
Bate, P., 76
Baumard, P., 46
Becher, T., 53

Berg, P.-O., 41, 42, 45, 46
Bergami, M., 19
Bergquist, W., 49
Beyer, J. H., 17, 44, 46, 60, 61, 64, 65, 71
Bhattacharya, C. B., 22
Biglan, A., 53
Birnbaum, R., 49, 50
Blackston, M., 30
Blau, P. M., 52
Bluedorn, A. C., 46
Bok, D., 7
Bolman, L., 50
Bolton, C. D., 50, 51
Bowen, H. R., 8, 40, 58
Branscombe, N. R., 23
Bresler, W., 58
Brickson, S., 22, 24
Broadfoot, L. E., 44
Brooks, S. M., 44
Brown, A. D., 19
Brown, J., 70
Burke, W. W., 76
Butler, C. L., 42

C

Calhoun, D., 20
Cameron, K. S., 41, 43, 48
Campbell, M. C., 28
Capella, L. M., 36
Carter, S. M., 17
Cartwright, S., 46
Chaffee, E. E., 47

Gouldner, A. G., 51
Grace, J. D., 36
Green, M., 76

H

Hall, D. T., 17, 20
Hall, J. E., 56
Hannah, D. R., 17
Hansen, C. D., 70
Harper, W. R., 69
Harquail, C. V., 3, 16, 17, 18, 19, 22, 24, 26, 33
Harris, L. C., 40, 72, 75
Harrison, A. W., 20
Hartley, M., 8, 14, 70, 76, 97
Hatch, M. J., 20, 57, 76
Hawkes, R. T., 58
Hearn, J., 36
Hedberg, B., 46
Helms Mills, J. C., 59
Heracleous, L., 44
Hermalin, B. E., 44
Heydinger, R., 36
Hill, B., 76
Hoeffler, S., 30
Hofstede, G., 42
Hogg, M. A., 22
Holcombe, K. M., 8, 40
Hollis, N. S., 30
Hopkins, M., 48
Horowitz, M., 34, 54, 66
Hummon, D. M., 65, 66
Humphreys, M., 19
Hurtado, S., 58

I

Iannozzi, M., 8
Itzin, C., 59

J

Jassawalla, A. R., 41
Jefferson, T., 69
Joachimsthaler, E., 27
Jones, G., 42
Jones, M. O., 64
Joyce, W. F., 61

K

Kafka, J. S., 71
Kahn, R. L., 50
Kahn, W. A., 20
Kamens, D. H., 72
Kammeyer, K.C.W., 50, 51
Kanter, R. M., 20
Kapferer, J.-N., 30, 35
Katz, D., 50
Keller, K. L., 17, 27, 28, 30, 31, 33, 35
Kennedy, A. A., 41, 46, 60, 65
Kerr, C., 51, 53, 54
Keyton, J., 70
Kezar, A. J., 76
Khan, R., 76
Kilduff, M., 44
Kimani, A., 33
Kramer, R. M., 20
Kuh, G. D., 6, 39, 40, 41, 42, 45, 47, 56, 57, 58
Kuhn, T., 21
Kunda, G., 20

L

Labianca, G., 7
Lakomski, G., 42
Larsen, M. H., 70
Lee, S., 30
Leslie, L. L., 36
Levinson, H., 20
Lewis, D., 46
Little, F., 70
Louis, M. R., 43, 57
Lund, D. B., 41
Lundberg, C. C., 43, 71, 76
Luthans, F., 42, 55

M

Mackay, M. M., 31
Mackey, A., 17
Madden, T. J., 33
Mael, F., 21, 22
Major, D. A., 58
Mallon, W., 76
Manning, K., 71
Maravelias, C., 46

Wilderom, C.P.M., 41, 44, 46
Wilensky, A. S., 70
Wiley, J. W., 44
Wilkins, A. L., 8, 41, 45, 70
Wilson, R. C., 52, 53
Wood, L., 28
Woodward, K., 20
Worline, M., 61
Wright, S., 42

Y

Yoo, B., 30

Z

Zammuto, R. F., 76
Zemsky, R., 8

Subject Index

A
Aaker's four-part model, 31–33
Adhocracy cultures, 48
Advantages, focusing on, 28–29
Advertising, 35
Affective commitment, 20
Anthropologists, 41, 42
Associations, brand, 31, 33

B
Brand associations, 31, 33
Brand awareness, 31, 32
Brand equity
    benefits of, 5
    building, 34–37
    defined, 2, 4, 30–31
    four features of, 31–33
Brand extension, 28
Brand loyalty, 31, 32
Brands
    defined, 28
    institutions as, 28–30

C
Clan cultures, 48
Climate, institutional, 8, 40
Collegial culture, 13, 49
Commencement ceremonies, 72–73
Community, concept of, 57–58
Continuance commitment, 20
Convocations, 72, 73
Culture. *See* Institutional culture

D
Developmental culture, 49
Disciplines that study culture, 41–44
Distinctiveness, 7, 8, 19, 20, 29, 57

E
Ethos of an institution, 57

F
Faculty subcultures, 52–53
Functionalist approach to research, 42, 43
Fundraising, 7, 14, 20, 24, 25, 28, 32

G
Gipp myth, 68

H
Hierarchy cultures, 48
Humor, campus-specific, 66–67

I
Identification. *See* Institutional
    identification
Identity, perceived organizational, 6, 15,
    17–18
Innovation, 35, 41
Institutional climate, 8, 40
Institutional culture
    defined, 2, 5–6, 39–41
    disciplinary foundations and, 41–44
    example illustrating, 8–14
    forms of, 59–74

About the Authors

J. Douglas Toma is associate professor of higher education at the Institute of Higher Education, University of Georgia, and dean of the Franklin Residential college.

Greg Dubrow is assistant professor of higher education in the Department of Educational Leadership and Policy Studies at Florida International University.

Matthew Hartley is assistant professor of higher education in the Policy, Management, and Evaluation Division at the Graduate School of Education, University of Pennsylvania.

About the ASHE Higher Education Reports Series

Since 1983, the ASHE (formerly ASHE-ERIC) Higher Education Report Series has been providing researchers, scholars, and practitioners with timely and substantive information on the critical issues facing higher education. Each monograph presents a definitive analysis of a higher education problem or issue, based on a thorough synthesis of significant literature and institutional experiences. Topics range from planning to diversity and multiculturalism, to performance indicators, to curricular innovations. The mission of the Series is to link the best of higher education research and practice to inform decision making and policy. The reports connect conventional wisdom with research and are designed to help busy individuals keep up with the higher education literature. Authors are scholars and practitioners in the academic community. Each report includes an executive summary, review of the pertinent literature, descriptions of effective educational practices, and a summary of key issues to keep in mind to improve educational policies and practice.

The Series is one of the most peer reviewed in higher education. A National Advisory Board made up of ASHE members reviews proposals. A National Review Board of ASHE scholars and practitioners reviews completed manuscripts. Six monographs are published each year and they are approximately 120 pages in length. The reports are widely disseminated through Jossey-Bass and John Wiley & Sons, and they are available online to subscribing institutions through Wiley InterScience (http://www.interscience.wiley.com).

Call for Proposals

The ASHE Higher Education Report Series is actively looking for proposals. We encourage you to contact one of the editors, Dr. Kelly Ward (kaward@wsu.edu) or Dr. Lisa Wolf-Wendel (lwolf@ku.edu), with your ideas.

Recent Titles

The Uses of Institutional Culture

Back Issue/Subscription Order Form

Copy or detach and send to:

Jossey-Bass, A Wiley Imprint, 989 Market Street, San Francisco CA 94103-1741

Call or fax toll-free: Phone 888-378-2537 6:30AM – 3PM PST; Fax 888-481-2665

Back Issues: Please send me the following issues at $24 each
(Important: please include series abbreviation and issue number.
For example AEHE 28:1)

_____

_____

_____

$ _____   **Total for single issues**

$ _____   SHIPPING CHARGES: SURFACE   Domestic Canadian

		Domestic	Canadian
	First Item	$5.00	$6.00
	Each Add'l Item	$3.00	$1.50

For next-day and second-day delivery rates, call the number listed above

Subscriptions   Please ❏ start ❏ renew my subscription to *ASHE-ERIC Higher Education Reports* for the year 2_____ at the following rate:

U.S.	❏ Individual $165	❏ Institutional $175
Canada	❏ Individual $165	❏ Institutional $235
All Others	❏ Individual $213	❏ Institutional $286

❏ Online subscriptions available too!

**For more information about online subscriptions visit
www.interscience.wiley.com**

$ _____   Total single issues and subscriptions (Add appropriate sales tax for your state for single issue orders. No sales tax for U.S. subscriptions. Canadian residents, add GST for subscriptions and single issues.)

❏Payment enclosed (U.S. check or money order only)

❏VISA ❏ MC ❏ AmEx ❏ #_____ Exp. Date _____

Signature _____ Day Phone _____

❏ Bill Me (U.S. institutional orders only. Purchase order required.)

Purchase order # _____

Federal Tax ID13559302   **GST 89102 8052**

Name _____

Address _____

Phone _____ E-mail _____

For more information about Jossey-Bass, visit our Web site at **www.josseybass.com**